TE MARAE

A Guide to
Customs & Protocol

Hiwi and Pat Tauroa

Photographs by Gil Hanly

T0363440

RAUPO

A RAUPO BOOK
Published by the Penguin Group, Penguin Group (NZ), 67 Apollo Drive, Rosedale,
North Shore 0632, New Zealand (a division of Pearson New Zealand Ltd)
Penguin Books Ltd, Registered Offices: 80 Strand, London, WC2R 0RL, England

First published by Reed Publishing (NZ) Ltd 1986
Reprinted 1987 (three times), 1988, 1990 (twice), 1992, 1993, 1997, 1998, 2000, 2001,
2002 (twice), 2003, 2004, 2005 (twice), 2006
New edition printed 2007

First published by Penguin Group (NZ) 2009
31 33 35 37 39 40 38 36 34 32

Printed in China through Asia Pacific Offset

ISBN: 978 0 14 320242 4

A catalogue record for this book is available from the National Library of New Zealand.
www.penguin.co.nz

Contents

Foreword

In many things
It is not well to say,
Know thyself,
It is better to say,
Know others.

Menander

Knowledge is the dawn of understanding. Understanding is the first sign of tolerance, and tolerance is the bright light of racial harmony. It was Frank Colby who once said, rather cynically, that "tolerance was composed of nine parts apathy to one of brotherly love". Unfortunately, apathy has been prevalent in New Zealand for far too long, and many, unwittingly or otherwise, have believed it to be the formula for racial understanding and tolerance.

The deliberate exodus of the Maori from their rural isolation into the urban community, for economic reasons, is a major factor of Maori evolution that has brought both races into closer contact and greater awareness of each other's cultural and racial differences. Each ethnic group has something to give the other and something to learn from each other.

Barriers are being created unnecessarily by the hypersensitivity of the Maori and the insensitivity of the Pakeha to Maori aspirations. But with goodwill, greater understanding, and better knowledge of each other's values and culture, these barriers can be demolished.

The authors, Pat and Hiwi Tauroa, have prepared much of the material for this book from their own childhood experiences on their home marae and from Hiwi's experiences as Race Relations Conciliator. Their efforts are an important endeavour to encourage cooperation and friendly values between Maori and non-Maori.

Maoritanga is the accepted word for Maori culture, which encompasses the whole Maori lifestyle – tribal living, behaviour, thought, feeling and experience, passed on from generation to generation. There is now taking place a resurgence of interest by the Maori in their own culture and a growing desire by fellow New Zealanders to know and experience it on the marae.

This work, then, is an extremely valuable contribution to race relations and will undoubtedly be recognised as important. Pat and Hiwi are well qualified by training and experience to help lay the foundations for a happier future, based on knowledge, respect and justice.

It is my great pride and pleasure, as Hiwi's fellow tribesman, to commend this book to as wide a readership as possible. May *Te Marae* reach every home throughout the land.

Kia hora te marino
Kia whakapapa pounamu te moana
Kia tere te karohirohi

May the seas be calm
May the shimmer of summer
Glisten like the greenstone
Dance across thy pathway

Jim Henare.

Sir James Henare
Moerewa, 1986

Acknowledgements

When we asked our kaumatua, "Why is it like this?" they replied, "Let me tell you the story of Taratara. You know when . . . "

In acknowledging the help received from various people with this book, we need first to acknowledge the learning and understanding that continues to be handed down by our tipuna. They taught by encouraging their listeners to "hear" and "see" beyond the spoken word and to understand how one thing is a partner of another. The young are made to look for an answer within their own understanding, so that, once they have understood, they apply their knowledge as a matter of course, as well as continuing to seek further understanding.

We acknowledge our kaumatua and kuia, from Ngapuhi and Ngai Tahu, who continue these traditions and add to them by helping and encouraging us and by giving us their support and confidence.

We acknowledge and are grateful also to te iwi o Waikato, who "adopted, sheltered and supported" us and helped us to better understand some of the tikanga of Waikato.

To those matua, whaea, kaumatua, rangatira, rangatahi and tamariki of Taranaki, Ngati Porou, Ngati Kahungunu, Ngaiterangi, Tuhoe, Te Arawa, Ngati Raukawa, Te Whanau-a-Apanui and all the tribal groups onto whose marae we have been welcomed – he mihi aroha ki a koutou katoa. We appreciate the help given by Joe Malcolm, Mita Mohi, "Aunty Rangi" Takarangi, Henry Bennett and Haare Williams. These people have helped to clarify some specific points of our understanding.

Warm thanks also to Ray Scott, who undertook the task of editing our writing to produce a helpful, informative document.

We are grateful for the support of the Visual Production Unit of the Department of Education in making the photograph on page 16 available to us. The diagrams by Rod Cooper are also acknowledged.

Finally, we thank our kaumatua Sir James Henare, who has encouraged, supported and guided us in our efforts to build a better understanding of what we are as spiritual people.

Introduction

Marae have been a part of the community scene in this country for centuries. During this time they have been the focal point of Maoridom. Marae kawa (customs and procedures) vary from one tribe to another. Despite this, Maori people are able to visit marae other than their own with confidence.

With the coming of the European, the situation changed. People unfamiliar with marae became participants. Some Europeans, by virtue of their office, found it necessary, or at least highly desirable, to conduct their business with the Maori on the familiar ground of their marae. In many cases it would have been the only possible meeting place, especially if the matter required discussion between representatives of different tribes. Such visitors were usually given sufficient instruction on marae protocol to enable them to visit without embarrassment. But, at other times, the Pakeha visitor would have responded to the unknown situation just as any person responds to a situation that is new and strange − with trepidation, fear or excitement.

During the last decade or so, urban Maori people have been returning frequently to their own marae – perhaps not to reside permanently, but at least to identify again with their roots. Rebuilding, adding new extensions, and carrying out general maintenance have continued at the home marae. This increased activity has been one major aspect of the rebirth of Maoritanga.

At the same time, increasing numbers of Pakeha and other non-Maori New Zealanders have been endeavouring to learn more about the culture of the original inhabitants of this country.

A culture cannot be learned from a textbook. True understanding and appreciation are possible only from first-hand experience. This has been recognised by both Maori and Pakeha; so, since many Pakeha people have expressed the desire to take part in a "marae experience", Maori people, aware of their sincerity, are now making special efforts to make marae more widely available to visitors seeking to learn.

Despite increasing numbers of Pakeha participating in marae activities, the Maori has made few concessions to the presence of non-Maori visitors. Maori people have chosen to maintain customs that they have developed and nurtured for many, many generations. It is essential for all New Zealanders that the Maori maintain the integrity of their culture rather than permit adjustments that are simply intended to make it easier for the non-Maori to fit in.

In order to prevent personal embarrassment and to avoid insulting one's hosts by saying or doing the wrong thing, it is necessary that a visitor know something of the basic ritual and procedures of a marae.

Most visitors will be keen to know the significance of the many customs that they have experienced or witnessed. There is no recipe for instant cultural understanding. To understand a culture requires a long period of learning. An essential ingredient is a continuing contact with the Maori people in a range of situations, particularly on the marae. For it is when gathered together on their marae that the Maori most fully express themselves as a people.

This book has been written to make the marae visit a more meaningful and rewarding experience. Although the visitor could possibly "get by" with a list of ten do's and don'ts, this book is for those who want to achieve more than just getting by.

To assist with learning, the ritual of the marae visit is divided into parts. Each part attempts to explain what is happening in a particular situation and why.

The rationales for some rituals are quite simple, practical and easily explained. Others are the result of deep feelings and beliefs, expressing Maori spirituality. These are not easy to explain, since they are based on activities and customs that span many generations.

It is hoped, however, that reading this book will enhance the experience of visitors to the marae, giving them a deeper feeling for, and appreciation of, one aspect of Maoridom.

As a prelude to the main section of the book, Hiwi Tauroa discusses the importance of his own tribal marae, Te Patunga, and visits to other marae during his upbringing. Some reminiscences go back to his boyhood.

Although it is comparatively easy to describe the components of marae and their functions, it is much more difficult, if not impossible, to describe the feelings that Maori have for their marae – their turangawaewae.

It is hoped that non-Maori readers will begin to glean some understanding of the real place of the marae in the life of an individual Maori, and some understanding of Maori spirituality, from this personal statement. It is included in the book because it illustrates a dynamic, living – albeit intangible – facet of Maoridom. To omit this facet would be to leave out what, to the Maori, is the major significance of the marae. The physical presence of a building is a tangible thing. Far more important to the Maori people are the intangible values that are embedded deeply in the spiritual significance of the buildings, in exchanges between people, and in the events that take place on the marae.

The word "marae" is both singular and plural. In the Maori language "s" is not added to form a plural. Many Maori words, however, have become part of the New Zealand English language and thus tend to be treated as English words. Most New Zealanders would refer to "one tui" but to "several tuis". Other words are in the process of transition, and "marae" is one such word. Most Maori people would now tend to speak of "several marae", but non-Maori people would probably say "several maraes". Following the preference of the Maori, the use of marae in both the singular and plural is advocated.

The whare nui, the whare kai, the church and the urupa all serve the needs of the community.

# *The marae in Maoridom* _____

What is this marae? Why do people gather here? What satisfactions do they gain when they come here? Why the fuss about building more marae? Is there something for the Pakeha on the marae? Why are increasing numbers of Pakeha, including tourists, visiting marae throughout the country – Hoani Waititi in Auckland, Otakou in Dunedin, Turangawaewae in Ngaruawahia, Waikohatu in Rotoiti, Nga Hau e Wha in Pukekohe, and Nga Hau e Wha in Christchurch?

These are straightforward questions, but the answers are not always simple. Yet to find just some of the answers is to start to understand the foundations of a culture. It is a culture that has been seriously at risk. If nourishment cannot flow from the roots to the leaves, the plant will die; if the nutrients of Maoridom cannot find expression upon the marae, then this culture will surely die.

The marae is the wahi rangatira mana (place of greatest mana), wahi rangatira wairua (place of greatest spirituality), wahi rangatira iwi (place that heightens people's dignity), and wahi rangatira tikanga Maori (place in which Maori customs are given ultimate expression).

The marae is that chiefly place where the heights of Maoridom and its values are expressed. Only in such a special place can the high levels of wairua (spirituality), mana (prestige), and tikanga (customs) be practised in their true setting. The marae is the place where people may stand tall. Here they are able to stand upon the Earth Mother and speak. Here they may express themselves, they may weep, laugh, hug and kiss. Every emotion can be expressed and shared with others – shared not only with the living but also with those generations who have gone ki tua o te arai (beyond the veil).

A marae needs people; people need a marae. People whose families become associated with caring and sharing contribute to the tradition of the marae. The tangata whenua (the people of the land, the hosts) are the unchanging foundation of a marae. Yet tangata whenua need manuhiri (visitors) – people for whom they can provide a service.

He aha te mea nui?	What is the greatest thing?
He tangata,	It is people,
He tangata,	It is people,
He tangata!	It is people!

Unfortunately, non-Maori people experience all the emotions that arise from ignorance of a situation known to have significance to another group. Negative emotional responses arise, just as they do in every situation that is not well understood. Whoever the people, there is fear of the unknown. Whoever the people, this fear expresses itself through responses that belittle, decry, reject or avoid that which is not understood.

For a century and a half, the Pakeha and others who share this country with the Maori have created organisations often designed to materially enrich themselves, hardly aware that within our society is an establishment capable of providing cultural and spiritual enrichment by service to others.

This is the marae. It is not just a place where people meet. It is the family home of generations that have gone before. It is the standing place of the present generation and will be the standing place for the generations to come. This spiritual aspect of the marae is its most important facet. Ko te marae taku turangawaewae (The marae is my standing place). It is the place where I have the right to stand before others and speak as I feel. While I am on my feet, I know that others will give me their respect and allow me to speak without interruption. In return, I shall extend to them the same courtesy when they speak, whether I agree or not.

For our people, marae are places of refuge that provide facilities to enable us to continue with our way of life within the total structure of Maoridom. We, the Maori, need our marae so that we may pray to God; rise tall in oratory; weep for our dead; house our guests; have our meetings, feasts, weddings and reunions; and sing and dance.

Maori who have no marae have no turangawaewae (standing place). They do not have the right and privilege of standing and speaking. They do not belong. Conversely, Maori who belong to a marae know that they have the right to stand and express their views on their marae. They know they have the right to be heard – that they belong.

Many Maori people are able to trace their ancestry and establish links with other tribal areas. Thus they have several turangawaewae.

This feeling of belonging cannot be adequately expressed in words. The customs, and respect for these customs, and the values reinforced by the wairua of the marae, give strength. Just as people wishing to express their religious beliefs will go to church or to a place of worship, so will Maori people seeking fulfilment and reaffirmation of their identity go to their marae. They will identify with it and learn from those who are there. This feeling of a need for identity cannot be expressed easily in words. The deeper feelings that are part of the hinengaro (mind or heart) are very real, yet they remain intangible. There is an awareness of one's heritage; an awareness that one is accepted. It is a place of security and comfort.

An analogy in the Pakeha world might be that of arriving home after a particularly busy and harrowing day. There is the sigh of relief – "thank goodness I'm home". You can put your feet up; the four walls and roof are yours. Everything is familiar: the faces, the surroundings, the noises, the conversation. At last you can truly relax. This is your home, and you belong.

Te marae, he tipuranga

GROWTH THROUGH THE MARAE

Recently I returned to the home of my people in Northland. The day after my arrival, I rose early in the morning, climbed a small hill, sat down, and soon felt the warming rays of the rising sun. I looked down onto the land of my people and onto our marae, Te Patunga. In one sense I was alone with my thoughts; in another sense there was an intangible association with those who had gone before and with the things of nature that they loved – an awareness of the partnership between people and their God. I easily recalled other marae, other whare, other people.

In my imagination I was standing again on the ground in front of the whare nui and rising to speak.

Te marae e takoto nei	The marae lying here
Tena koe	I greet you

Papatuanuku te whaea	Papatuanuku the Earth Mother
Tena koe	I greet you
I ahau e tu ake nei	While I stand here
Ka huri oku whakaaro	My thoughts turn
Ki a ratou, oku tipuna	To them, my ancestors
I tu ake hoki i nga wa o mua.	Those who also stood in years gone by.

While I stand here on you, Mother Earth, I feel safe, for I know that on this very place others have stood before me – my ancestors. They stood here; they wept here; they planned here; they responded to the karanga (call of welcome); they experienced the powhiri (the welcome itself); they exchanged greetings and thoughts. My father, my grandfather and his father – they stood then as I do now. We honour you, Mother Earth; by you all life is sustained; you give us food; from you grow the forest trees – they share their seeds; from you springs the harakeke (flax) from which we make our baskets; from you come the dyes that colour our artifacts and houses.

From the children of Tane – the trees – we have been able to draw fire. And Tane's other children – the birds – find food and branches in which to nest and multiply.

Our bodies will return to you again; it is you who will guard them and use them as you will. Mother Earth, how proud we are to be your trustees during our lifetime. Just as our ancestors gifted you to us, so may we gift you to future generations, that they may share with you and care for you.

Marae-atea, representative of Mother Earth, we share life and death with you. How clearly I see my people stamping on you in haka – "Ka eke ki te wiwi" – sharing among themselves, and with you, their pride and their confidence. I hear, too, the bell tolling as my kuia (grandmother) is taken away – ki tona okiokinga (to her resting place). I hear the wailing; I can picture the hupe (mucus) and roimata (tears) falling, for I also cried here for my father. I know that you have absorbed the roimata of my people.

Marae-atea, you could never be for me just a piece of clay, or dirt, or grass. You are, indeed, to those of us who are gathered here, a sacred place.

Overlooking the marae-atea is my spiritual home, my whare tipuna (ancestral house). I salute you again, as I have done before.

Te whare e tu ake nei	The house standing there
Tena koe, tena koe, tena koe.	Greetings, greetings, greetings.
I te wao nui o Tane koe e tu ana	In times past you stood in the forest of Tane
Kati, inaianei, ko	But, now, you bring people and bind them
Tane-whakapiripiri koe.	together.
Ta tatou whare tipuna	Our house, spanning the generations,
Tu tonu, tu tonu.	Continues to stand.

How stirring yet how comforting is the karanga of the kuia (older woman), just as it beckoned my ancestors before me. My father came to this marae often; he stood where his father stood before him: my children come with the same feeling of reverence and the same thoughts of tapu (sacredness). My mokopuna (grandchildren) will also come here; they will respond to the karanga and the powhiri. Generations that I will know nothing of will follow them.

Here I am, walking slowly towards you, whare tipuna. And I know this: I am not I, but we; whare tipuna, you are not you, but they. I pause before you and bow in respect, not just to those who have gone before, but to all those who share your mana now. And I pay silent homage to those who will share with you the welfare of nga whakatupuranga e heke mai nei (the generations to come).

You, my kaumatua (elders), my whaea (mothers), my matua (parents), who sit in your special place – I do not see only you, for I see the same gestures and expressions, and I hear the same voices, as those who have sat there before you.

Whare tipuna, in you are all the thoughts, knowledge, emotions and love of our people. And, if we are to share these things with you, you must speak to us. I look at you and think of your kin on other marae. Some are carved and painted. You are not. Yet, like you, they also live. The tekoteko, the ancestor, will sit there above. On all marae your arms are always extended to greet me. As I look through the open door and see the length of your body, I know how important it is to you that the door be open. How could you possibly beckon people to you while closing your door and denying entry? The tangata whenua know this and have called to this generation that all generations are welcome.

Haeremai,	Welcome,
Haeremai,	Welcome,
Haeremai.	Welcome.

Each visitor is thrice welcome.

I know by the width and the length of your arms that they are all-embracing and that your back is also very strong. Like your ancestor represented in the tekoteko, the back must be strong, for you must continue to stand, to resist the elements, and to be a sign of strength and permanence.

I know that within you stand the poupou – the carved symbols representing our close ancestors. I know that tonight I will choose to sleep as close to my own poupou as possible, though my kaumatua will have first choice of place.

I know that between your poupou are the tukutuku panels woven by our women. They represent the foundations of our spirituality: the whetu rangi, associating us with the stars; the niho taniwha, representing strength; the arawhata, leading us to the spiritual heaven; and the patiki, representing the food that is essential for our physical wellbeing.

I know that your ribs are decorated and that the kowhaiwhai patterns on them are both beautiful and meaningful, joining the ancestors from one side of the house with those from the other.

And I know that your feet are firmly planted on Mother Earth, as are the feet of the children of Tane Mahuta, the trees. You stand now, as did Tane Mahuta then, keeping the Sky Father, Ranginui, separated from the Earth Mother, Papatuanuku, so that we may have light and life.

Tonight, whare tipuna, we who honour you will be protected by you. We will talk and laugh and then sleep in peace. From the poupou (carved panels), from the tahuhu (ridgepole), from the pou tokomanawa (central carved post), there will softly descend upon us the cloak of our ancestors. We will be protected, as only they can protect us. There is no greater warmth than that passed on to us by those who have gone before us. There is no greater peace than that which our ancestors confer upon us.

No, you are not just a house. You live; and because you live we can live. And as we pour our warmth, our love, and our peace into your timbers, into your designs, into your body, so may we draw from you a greater share of love. And you will give love and protection to the generations who will shelter within you, long after I am called by Hine-nui-te-po (Goddess of Death). It is your presence that tells us that we still live. If you collapse and fall, we have failed you and we shall surely die.

E te whare tipuna,	Ancestral house,
E tu, e tu. Tu tonu.	Stand, stand. Continue to stand.
Ake tonu atu.	Forever.

Standing on its own is the whare kai (dining room).

| Ko te tohu o te marae | The sign of a wealthy marae |
| Ko te pataka . . . | Is its pataka (food store) . . . |

When, as a child, I was taken onto our marae, I was given the task of cutting and carrying wood for the fire. It was a wide fireplace with a corrugated-iron chimney. Stretched across the chimney was a blackened water pipe, and hanging from the pipe were lengths of number-eight fencing wire bent up at the ends. True to their fish-hook appearance, the wires had caught a number of blackened billies, kerosine tins, and large iron pots. Other iron pots stood on pieces of railway line.

I spent many hours watching the older people sitting, testing the food, playing cards, drying tea towels, gossiping, and passing family news. To us youngsters, it was pretty boring. But our pakeke (adults) seemed to enjoy it. Even when they didn't seem to need to boil water, they boiled it. There seemed no need for the big fires they built, but they built them. And when some of them left and said, "Hey kids, keep an eye on the fire and the kai (food)", we really felt good. There was no real need to lift the lid and stir the water, but we stirred it – and felt important. Now that we weren't being ordered to fetch more ti-tree, we fetched it, and burned it.

We used to watch the men kill the pig. They would stab it – only once. I didn't like the blood but made out that it didn't worry me. Then the time came when I was asked to help set up the hangi and, eventually, to help cut up the meat. I really felt good then.

One day I got growled at for taking a piece of pork rind and eating it when I should have been helping to serve the meal. "You feed the manuhiri first," I was told. "Learn to wait – we eat last." Most times, eating last was pretty good anyway.

Whare kai, I remember my apprenticeship with you – washing and drying never-ending pots and plates. I hated doing those things at home and would do anything to dodge them. But here with you it was different; somehow we felt proud to do these things. The more dishes we dried, the better we felt.

Whare kai, you are a symbol of service to others; and, from your shared acts of service, mana is bestowed. As people working with you become exhausted, their energy is renewed by turning to your close friend, neighbour and relation – the whare tipuna. It is here that the strength of the ancestor is poured into the exhausted body. So, for generations to come, you two will work together – within you, te whare tipuna; within you, te whare kai.

Te whare kai e tu ake nei,	Dining room standing here,
Tena koe, tena koe, tu tonu.	Greetings, greetings, continue to stand.

Nearby is the whare karakia (church).

Tama ngakau marie	Son of peace
Tama a te Atua	Son of God
Tenei tonu matou	We here in this place
Arohaina mai.	Seek your love.

Sometimes we wondered about the Christian message. We wondered why, at certain times, we had to stop playing, dress up, and go to church. As we grew older, we started to understand what the church was about. Yet I wonder whether it ever took the place of the whare tipuna. We enjoyed services in the meeting house. We knew of the poupou; we liked to sit on the mattresses, sometimes remembering that our old people before us had sat there too. We felt better standing as we were – some dressed up, some in old clothes, some wrapped in blankets. We just liked it that way, and God seemed to be right there with us. We seemed to get more feeling from our hymns, somehow. Nobody seemed to need to growl.

I was married in you, whare karakia. Some of my family got married in front of the whare tipuna. My dad used to whai korero (speak) there, just as he used to preach in you.

I remember sitting on a hill with my dad. He was explaining that God is everywhere and that God loves everyone. He was trying to make me understand that in respecting Tane Mahuta (God of Trees), Tangaroa (God of the Sea) and all the other gods of Maoridom, we are respecting the things that have been given to us by God. He told me also of many of the old Maori proverbs that have an equivalent in Christianity.

Whare karakia, I respect you and I take comfort from your presence. Quite often, when no one else is with you, I come in and sit on a seat. And, when I leave you, I look at the hand bell by the door and hope that it will always be there to go on calling people to worship. I used to think that someone was bound to pinch it, but they haven't yet. I hope that one day my children will pick it up and ring it and call their children into your presence.

| Whare karakia | House of God |
| Tu tonu, tu tonu | Stand, stand. |

Finally, my eyes come to rest on the urupa (cemetery) and I recall the words on Dad's headstone.

Ki a ratou	To them
Te kotahi anake;	He was only one;
Ki a matou	To us, the family,
Ko ra te ao katoa.	He was the whole world.

People express themselves in different ways. Sadness and loss and pain are not emotions that are restricted to one family, one tribe, or one people. Life and death are as inevitable as day and night. As night follows day, so death must follow life. But night becomes day again; life survives death.

Te po; te po.	It's dark; it's dark.
Te ao; te ao.	It's light; it's light.

Each headstone within the urupa faces east. Those who lie there acknowledge the rising sun. And for the whole day, until te tonga o te ra (the setting of the sun), the dead experience its rays; it rises at the feet and sets at the head. I like to wander among the headstones. I see the name Wairongo, my father's twin brother. I remember when he died. I see two more headstones with the names of Hariata and Himiona; Hariata was my tipuna whaea (grandmother), Himiona was my tipuna matua (grandfather). Your headstones are getting harder to read.

And, Dad, I look at your headstone there with your family. I think I know, now, why Mum wants to go back to lie with her sisters, brothers and taua (grandmother) instead of lying in this wahi tapu (sacred place) where you are. She feels the call of her kainga-tupu – the place where she was born and raised. She would like to be with you, but you are her only family here. The call to return to her own home in Ngai Tahu is now very strong for her.

Papatuanuku, take care of my family. They live in me, just as they lie in you.

Te wahi tapu, te urupa,	The sacred place, the cemetery,
Takoto tonu.	Lie still.
Te hunga mate	The dead
ki te hunga mate;	we leave with the dead;
Te hunga ora	The living
ki te hunga ora.	we unite with the living.
Tena koutou, tena koutou,	Greetings, greetings,
Tena tatou katoa.	Greetings to us all.

Organising a marae visit

HOW TO ARRANGE A VISIT

Unfortunately, there is no single, simple procedure that can be outlined. Apart from the Office of the Race Relations Conciliator* in Auckland, there are only a few organisations that will arrange visits for individuals. On the other hand, any group, using a little initiative and a good deal of humility, should be able to contact people in their community who have ready access to a marae.

In the case of school parties, one of the teachers should contact the marae committee, preferably through a friend or mutual acquaintance. One member of the committee is usually responsible for marae bookings. Many marae are listed by name in the telephone book. Business firms, professional groups, and social or cultural organisations should probably follow the same procedure.

*P.O. Box 6163, Wellesley Street, Auckland; telephone (09) 307-2352.

It is rather more difficult for an individual to arrange a personal visit, but several options are open. You could contact a Maori person living in the area and seek his or her help.

Again, you could walk onto a marae quietly and respectfully, remembering that it is not a public place, and seek out a person who may be willing to help.

If a group is already assembled to go onto a marae, you could "tag on" and thus gain legitimate entry, for all are welcome to attend any function on a marae.

Finally, marae always seem to be short of helpers to do general maintenance work. An offer to help would probably be gratefully accepted, providing both an introduction and an entry.

However, it is essential that your desire to learn is a genuine one, not just an inquisitive wish to see what happens on the marae. Sincerity will be felt by the tangata whenua (people of the marae); lack of sincerity will also be felt, and this could lead to a visitor being embarrassed and frustrated by being "held at arm's length".

MARAE ORGANISATION

It may appear that a marae is not well organised, because it seems impossible to identify anyone as the "boss". No one seems to be the main leader all the time, and very few orders are given – except, perhaps, "Haere mai ki te kai" ("Come and eat"). To the visitor, it seems amazing that hundreds of people can so easily be welcomed, fed and cared for, with the minimum of fuss and bother.

How, then, does a marae "come alive"? How does it give the impression that there is no hustle and bustle during the course of a hui?

Every marae has a committee that functions like most other committees set up for a specific purpose. There is normally a chairperson, a secretary and/or treasurer, and associated members. Visitors wishing to attend a marae would normally contact the secretary or chairman of the marae committee.

The purpose of the marae committee is to organise the marae before, during and after an event. Most importantly, committee members are charged with maintaining the mana of the marae. The work is time-consuming and, significantly, performed voluntarily. It is the Maori values of manaaki (caring for), aroha (love) and turangawaewae (a place to belong) that motivate the hosts to continue this work.

There are simple, well-established rules that sustain the procedures of the marae. The kawa (protocol) should be understood before a marae visit. It is important that groups be well prepared before participating in a formal visit. There are normally "experts" in the local community who will be willing to brief groups in advance. The reading of this or any other book will not be sufficient. It is impossible to give information here on the traditions and history of a particular marae, the names of the elders of that marae, the name of the particular whare tipuna, or the specific form of kawa pertaining to that particular marae. These aspects all vary from one marae to another.

WHAT IS NEEDED ON A MARAE

Mattresses and pillows are provided for an overnight stay. So, too, are pillow slips and a sheet that covers the mattress. Visitors should each bring their own blankets or sleeping bag. Comfortable clothing and night attire should be included, as well as socks and slip-on shoes (for easy removal). Obviously, toilet gear should be included, together with a towel and additional clothing appropriate to the season. This may include a jersey, raincoat or sun hat.

Money will also be needed for the koha (gift). This is discussed more fully on page 82.

WHAT TO DO WHEN GOING TO THE MARAE

Through schools, through friendships, through intermarriage, and through an increasing desire to learn and appreciate Maori values, Pakeha people are becoming more and more familiar with the marae. This is good. But it is most important that the Pakeha accept those aspects of the marae that are valuable to the Maori, rather than disregarding them or attempting to introduce Pakeha substitutes for them. Likewise, Maori people should ensure that those aspects of the marae that give them pride and confidence are respected, and that both they and their visitors retain and practise the traditional customs.

It is only human to feel apprehensive when faced with a new and different experience.

It is understandable, therefore, that Pakeha people are often fearful of their first visit to a marae. In addition, they may be reluctant to stay overnight. It is hoped that the following sections of the book will help to allay some of these fears.

The majority of Pakeha people do not understand the language and the kawa of the marae. They are understandably concerned that, quite unintentionally, they may do or say something that could offend. Full understanding of a marae cannot be expected after one visit. The marae represents people – it takes time to get to know people and to appreciate their feelings and beliefs.

On the marae

TANGATA WHENUA / HOSTS ON THE MARAE

The tangata whenua are the local people who, by descent and nowadays by association, have a turangawaewae (situational identity) with the marae. Their turangawaewae gives them the right to participate in determining the kawa of the marae; to determine what functions can be held and when they might best be held; to define roles on the marae; and to ensure that hospitality is provided to others. Being tangata whenua prescribes their responsibilities and obligations to visitors. Their basic task is to prepare for visitors, to ensure that they are well fed and cared for, and to ensure that, whatever the kaupapa (reason) for the hui (meeting), it is a success. They contribute to the food supplies, provide the work force for the kitchen, dining room, meeting house and grounds, and welcome the visitors. It is the tangata whenua who remove the tapu from the visitors to allow them to become one with the tangata whenua.

For the duration of the visit, visitors are given some of the privileges and responsibilities of tangata whenua. They are now free to move on any part of the marae. They may help the ringa wera ("hot hands"; workers) in the kitchen with their chores, assist in welcoming further visitors, or become one of those invited to sit on the paepae (speakers' platform).

This tangata whenua status is an honorary one, for first-time visitors especially, and applies for the duration of that particular hui. It is not carried away with the visitor when he or she leaves the marae. However, it does mean that the visitor is no longer a waewae tapu (sacred foot, or first-time visitor to that particular marae) and could therefore go to that marae at some future time without needing to be formally welcomed.

The tangata whenua can be divided into subgroups on the basis of their hosting roles, even though the roles will overlap. These subgroups comprise young children, teenagers, adults and elders.

Young children have access to all parts of the marae. They can play anywhere on the marae; but, when a formal welcome is in progress on the marae-atea, this becomes out of bounds. Children, like everyone else, are valued members of the marae. .They belong to the marae and are important. All adults on the marae become "parents" to these children, and it is the responsibility of all adults to care for them and to discipline them if necessary.

Teenagers also have considerable freedom on the marae. They, too, learn by experience. They are expected to carry seats, set and clear tables, serve meals, pour coffee or tea, wash and dry dishes, and generally do manual work to ensure that visitors are looked after. They help the ringa wera.

Adults are the ringa wera. On them depends the mana of their marae. Food has to be ordered and delivered; fires have to be tended (where appropriate); meals have to be prepared, cooked and served; the hangi has to be put down. Gardens have to be maintained; buildings, including the ablution block, have to be kept clean; and the whare moe (sleeping house) must be make ready for the manuhiri.

The fourth important group is nga kaumatua (the elders, both men and women). It is very difficult to define when a person becomes an elder, as distinct from an adult. Some elders are experts in the area of whakapapa (genealogy); others are more expert in whai korero; some older woman excel in waiata (song); others are experts in karanga.

In some districts where there are very few older folk, the younger group of men and women assume the role of elders. In other areas, where the number of elders is greater, the older leaders may be very old, so the younger ones have to wait "in the wings" until given the opportunity to participate in the formal arena. This may become frustrating to some of the more impatient youth.

A feature of marae life is that there is always a place for the old people – both male and female. The mana and authority of the elders are very influential, yet inconspicuous. They are honoured because of their wisdom, their wise counsel, their expertise in nga taonga a nga tipuna (treasures of the ancestors), and their authority in matters pertaining to the marae. Their role is to "front" the marae, to welcome the visitors, to ensure that the kawa is followed, and, when questioned specifically, to pass their knowledge on to the young.

In all these roles, the Maori is expected to learn by seeing, by hearing, and by doing. Rarely is he or she specifically told what to do or why it should be done. The expectation is that by seeing their elders in action, young people know how things should be done. So, when it is time for them to assume that role, they know exactly what is expected and how to respond.

TE HUIHUINGA KI WAHO / THE GATHERING TOGETHER

The organisers of a hui usually suggest that those persons wishing to enter the marae, should gather together outside the marae gates by a certain time. This is not a request that is made of Pakeha people only. When going to a tangi (funeral) or hui, it is expected that, unless they are arriving in a large group, visitors will wait at least a few minutes. This is to make sure that there is not another group of manuhiri already being welcomed on the marae, and to see if other individuals also arrive. Of course, if a group does arrive, one could join that group. It is most helpful to the tangata whenua if visitors enter as a combined group. This lessons the burden on the speakers and on the ringa wera in the whare kai.

While gathering together, it is usual to greet all others at the gate, whether they are known to you personally or not. A hariru (handshake) is right and proper. Should the other people waiting be well known to you, then there will follow the hongi (pressing of noses), and kiss and hug, and maybe even tears.

The manuhiri stand in the gateway to the marae, indicating that they are waiting for the karanga (call of welcome).

Speakers for the manuhiri will be selected. The person selected as the last speaker for the group will place the koha, usually money, on the marae. One person will collect the koha while the group is outside the gate. If you are alone among strangers, ask one of them who the last speaker is to be, and give your koha to that person. This is a very personal gift. A note or notes, folded up or placed in an envelope (with your name on the outside if you want it recorded), is acceptable. It is not good form to show others at the gate the amount that you propose to give. It is not usual, either, to enquire as to what the koha should be. This is your personal decision. You give what you, personally, wish to give.

During this time of gathering together, smoking and talking quietly are part of the "settling down" process. Loud calling, boisterous behaviour, and children playing chase do not contribute to the state of mind that is appropriate on such a tapu occasion. Neither would loud noise be appreciated by those on the marae, especially if a group were in the process of being welcomed.

When the tangata whenua are ready, one of them usually approaches the visitors waiting outside and indicates that the tangata whenua are ready.

The order in which the group assembles at the gate depends on the local kawa. In some areas all the men precede the women, and the speakers and most important menfolk will be expected to be in front. In other areas the important menfolk will be in front, followed by the women, the children and the other men, who may form themselves to the sides and rear of the body of womenfolk. Again, the group could be led on by the womenfolk, with those men who will be speaking to the side of the group of woman. Sometimes the kai whakautu (woman who will respond to the karanga) will be in front of the group and lead them on; at other times she will be to the side or slightly behind the leading male members. Those who will whai karero (speak) and waiata should be to the fore of the group.

Before entering the gate, talking and smoking cease. Once the manuhiri begin to move forward in response to the karanga, or the wero if it is issued, they do so in a respectful way and as a body. It is not good practice to "hang back", no matter how strong the inclination.

TE WERO / THE CHALLENGE

"Wero" literally means "to cast a spear", and it is a challenge that is accorded to distinguished visitors. Originally, the purpose of the wero was to find out whether the visiting party came in peace or in war.

As with all other aspects of the marae, the basic principles are universal, but there are differences in detail between one tribe and another and for different occasions. There is significance in the way that the taiaha (spear) is held and swung and there is significance in the way that the taki (challenge dart) – which may be a small carved dart or a twig – is placed before the manuhiri.

The wero is always issued by a male, who will begin his "intimidation" from the ranks of the tangata whenua before the karanga is issued. Thus the manuhiri must stand at the

Taua (warriors) stand ready to issue the wero (challenge); the kai karanga and tangata whenua are in readiness; empty seats are set out for the manuhiri.

gate and wait until the opportunity arises to show that their intentions are peaceful. This they will do by their most honoured member picking up the taki. A wero may be issued to a woman of rank – such as the Queen – but the taki must always be picked up by a male member of her party.

On a full ceremonial occasion there are three challengers. The first is the rakau whakaara (warning challenger). If he believes that the manuhiri have come in peace, he places the taki parallel to the manuhiri; if he places the taki with the point towards the group, he believes that they have come for war. If he throws the taki at them – he could be asking for trouble.

When the taki has been picked up, the second challenger – the rakau takoto – comes forward to prevent the manuhiri from advancing further until the rakau whakaara has returned to the chief with the information that he has gleaned. His taki is placed in the peaceful position. As he returns to the tangata whenua, always facing the manuhiri, the third challenger – the rakau whakawaha – proceeds to challenge the manuhiri. When his taki is picked up, he turns his back on the manuhiri and brings his taiaha over his head with the point towards the marae – the signal for the manuhiri to come forward. The karanga and the powhiri then begin.

On some occasions the rakau whakawaha may place his taki in the warlike position and, at the end of his wero, slap his thigh and run for the security of his people. The manuhiri, having been challenged, may send one of their number to chase and, if possible, to ground the challenger. This caused some consternation at the Waitangi Day ceremony in 1985 when a young naval "warrior" from the Governor General's party caught and grounded the challenger. Protesters present – not immediately understanding the full significance of what was happening – became momentarily irate. The young challenger was mortified that he had got cramp at a most awkward time.

The full significance of the wero stems from the traditional need of the marae to determine the intent of their manuhiri. This was done without any physical contact between the tangata whenua and the manuhiri. It was done through a spiritual awareness of the actions of people and the responses between people. The taki, the representative of Tane Mahuta, is placed before you, to invite you to come in peace, while recognising that you may have a take (reason) for which harsh words may need to be spoken. However, on the marae-atea a way can always be found whereby an exchange of words, of wairua (spirit) and of feelings can bring people to a better understanding of one another. By accepting the wero, you take the first step signifying the beginning of an exchange between people. Relaxation results from the knowledge that, for the time being, we are at peace one with another.

TE KARANGA / THE CALL

As soon as the tangata whenua see that the manuhiri are ready to proceed, a woman – the kai karanga (the caller) will karanga (call). Although there is a recognised pattern for karanga, their composition will vary according to the kai karanga and the occasion.

The kai karanga calls her
welcome.

In most cases the karanga will incorporate a welcome to the particular marae, both to the manuhiri and to the spirits of the dead. A typical one may take this pattern:

Haere mai ra	Come forward
Nga manuhiri tuarangi e	Visitors from afar
Haeremai, haeremai.	Welcome, welcome.
Mauria mai o koutou tini mate	Bring with you the spirits of your dead
Kia mihia	That they may be greeted
Kia tangihia e.	That they may be mourned.
Piki mai, kake mai,	Ascend onto our marae,
Whakaekea mai te marae tapu	Ascend the sacred marae
O te iwi e.	Of our people
Haeremai, haeremai, haeremai.	Welcome, welcome, welcome.

The manuhiri will then move silently onto the marae as one body. The group should remain as close together as possible. It is poor taste to gaze around at the view or at the people on the marae.

A woman from the visiting group – a kai whakautu – will return the karanga on behalf of the manuhiri. Each group honours the other. They also pay homage to those whom they represent, those who have gone before.

Maori people hold to the tradition that the karanga is sacred and makes a very special contribution to the marae. The karanga constitutes the first words spoken between tangata whenua and manuhiri. It is the first expression of welcome. It is the way by which the tangata whenua first make contact with the manuhiri, across the physical space that exists between the two groups. The karanga provides a safe word pathway, along which the manuhiri may pass without fear.

Just as the ancestors live on through the house, so the karanga provides the medium by which the living and the dead of the manuhiri may cross the physical space to unite with the living and the dead of the tangata whenua.

The karanga can be issued only by the women. Without the karanga, visitors remain outside the marae at the gate. It is the women, then, among the tangata whenua, who provide the first "key" to entry. The "key" is a spiritual one – the karanga. Only when the karanga has been issued by the tangata whenua can the group safely move onto the marae.

Except in exceptional instances, it is also a woman from among the visitors who first accepts the offer of the "key" in her karanga whakautu (call in reply). It is usual for a group of men to ensure that they are accompanied by at least one woman to a marae. Sometimes visitors will wait outside the gate until a woman arrives, so that there can be a response to the host's karanga. Should there not be a person able to respond in karanga among the manuhiri, this should not be a cause for embarrassment. Such is the aroha of the people that, if it is known that no one from the manuhiri is able to respond in karanga to the host's karanga, a tangata whenua will come to the gate and join the visitors. This happens especially if the manuhiri is a group of men of some standing.

Thus, while a woman is not entitled to take part in the whai korero section of the welcome, in most tribal areas she dictates when or whether the visitors will be called onto the marae. Without the karanga there can be no powhiri.

Over recent years, at the Waitangi marae, the tangata whenua decided that the mana of their marae had been trampled on so often by certain groups that they would not, in future, welcome them onto the marae. There were kaumatua present who could have, and would have, sat on the paepae, but because the womenfolk would not issue a karanga, there could be no whai korero exchange.

The karanga is not just the call of one person to another. It is a spiritual call. The kai karanga, through her call, represents the host of people who, in the same way and in the same kind of situation, have called throughout the generations.

The karanga carries with it the mana of the marae. Consequently. the woman who is the kai karanga for the tangata whenua, or the kai whakautu for the manuhiri, is very conscious of the responsibilities she holds. Her call is for her marae, her hapu (extended family), and her iwi (tribe).

Sometimes there will be as many as three separate kai karanga to call the manuhiri onto the marae. In other areas the kai karanga call the group onto the marae and then directly into the whare nui.

The karanga whakautu, the responding karanga from the manuhiri, should include advice to the tangata whenua as to who is in the group and where it is from. Sometimes it is possible to refer to the reason for the coming of the visitors. If it is for a tangi, the karanga whakautu refers to the tupapaku (deceased); if it is for a wedding, the karanga could refer to the occasion and perhaps trace an earlier ancestral marriage. Further information thought to be important might be passed across the space between the two groups by two or three kai karanga.

Not all women learn to karanga, and it would be most unusual for formal lessons to be held in the art of karanga. The question has been asked, "Why are there not recorded lessons for those who want to learn to karanga?" There are two main reasons for this. Firstly, the karanga is more than a call — it is a manifestation of many emotions, and it is not possible to teach feelings. The karanga is an expression of emotion. It is true that there are basic calls and responses, but in calling and responding to a karanga, the feelings expressed are a major ingredient. There will be feelings for the marae, for the tangata whenua, for the manuhiri, and for the tipuna (ancestors), as well as the personal feelings of the kai karanga herself.

Secondly, the kai karanga is always a woman. In most cases she is a kuia of the group or marae. Younger women will generally not karanga when there is an older woman present, unless the older woman asks the younger person to do so. Even today, most women will not karanga while they are menstruating, because of the tapu that is associated with this act. Many young women will not karanga while their grandmother, mother and/ or elder sister are still living, unless these older relatives have given their teina (younger relative) the right to karanga. If this right is given to a younger woman, the price is very high. By granting the younger woman the right to karanga, older relatives can give away, sometimes for ever, their right to karanga, especially on their own marae. Young women do not, therefore, ask their tipuna or elders to allow them to karanga. Should this younger person never offer the mana of the older woman back to her, and arrogantly revel in her personal karanga skills, she will destroy the mana of the kuia among her people. Years of attendance at marae, years of listening, will ultimately prepare a woman for the role of kai karanga.

The karanga is a call in Maori that invites you to whakaeke mai (come forward) bringing with you also, through you, your ancestors. It invites the manuhiri to bring the memories of their dead with them. Thus the loved ones of the manuhiri who have died may meet with the loved ones of the tangata whenua who have also passed ki tua o te arai (beyond the veil). So, as the hunga ora (the living) meet together, so too do the hunga mate (the dead).

The karanga awakens the emotions. It brings an awareness that what is happening is not just a simple act of going onto a marae – there is a presence of people, both physical and spiritual. The whole procedure of coming together is based on a tradition that is as meaningful today as it was in the past.

TE POWHIRI / THE WELCOME

A powhiri is not invariably "performed" for every group of manuhiri who go onto a marae. It is often reserved for special visitors or for tupapaku (the arrival of the body of the deceased) for a tangihanga (funeral). Each marae determines if and when it will "perform" the powhiri.

On some occasions the powhiri begins before the karanga; at other times it begins after the karanga has started. At some point the karanga and the powhiri will be taking place at the same time.

For the powhiri, the kai karanga usually stands to the side and slightly to the front of the remainder of the tangata whenua. Those who take part in the powhiri include elders (men and women) and young people – in fact, all who are on the marae at the time of the visitors' arrival and are free to take part.

Most often, and especially when there is a tupapaku, the tangata whenua will hold a small twig of green leaves in each hand. These twigs – or the hands if no twigs are being held – are shaken continuously, especially while they are in the upright position. The green leaves represent te ao, te po (light and darkness, or life and death). These two are contrasted in the light underside and the dark upper surface of the leaves.

When the powhiri is being performed, the tangata whenua stand and move their hands in unison to touch the thighs, before raising their hands until they are slightly above the head. This action is repeated in time to a chant that is most often called by a kaumatua.

Leader	People	
Toia mai,	te waka	Pull up, the canoe
Kumea mai,	te waka	Drag up, the canoe
Ki te urunga,	te waka	To the resting place, the canoe
Ki te moenga,	te waka	To the sleeping place, the canoe

All

Ki te takotoranga i   To the place where it will lie

Takoto ai, te waka.   At rest, the canoe.

The powhiri serves to ward off any evil spirits that may be present, ensuring a safe passage for the visitors across the marae space to their seats. The continuous movements of the hands and twigs remind the people of the presence of Tawhirimatea, the God of the Winds. As Tawhirimatea breathes, the leaves on the trees shake. As they shake, the light underside appears, then the dark upper surface. The stronger the breathing of the God of Winds, the more the light and dark play together. So, as the wind blows through the children of Tane Mahuta, the fingers of the children shake and bend. The leaves remind us that life is linked with death; that life and death are interwoven. As we gather on the marae, we bring the spirits of our dead with us. And in both life and death is the continuous presence of God.

The call of the powhiri likens the arrival of the group of visitors to the safe arrival of a canoe, with its paddlers and passengers, to the shore. The canoe is dragged safely to a resting place on the shore. Now the people are able to celebrate their arrival with food, having first observed some important customs. Likewise, the voices of the powhiri symbolically represent the tow rope by which visitors are pulled safely onto the marae. So, from the gates, the rope-plaited voice of the kai karanga intertwines and twists to give greater strength to the voices of the powhiri, strengthened still further by tears of memory and the karanga whakautu. All who are participating are protected by the tapu of the marae. As long as there are people and the marae, the rope represented by the voices of people is a rope that ties and pulls people together. It stretches from the past, appears in the present, and disappears to serve future generations.

As the chanting ends, the hands are held in the upright position – trembling still – until the kaumatua calls "tukua iho" or "ki raro", when the hands are lowered. If green twigs have been used, these are gathered into a container or put somewhere out of the way behind the paepae. The gathering together of the twigs is carried out without any undue fuss while the manuhiri are seating themselves. The leaves remain in the state of tapu that exists while visitors are going onto the marae. When the process of welcoming the manuhiri is over, the leaves, like the people, will become noa (common).

TE WHAKAEKENGA / THE GOING ON

Group leaders proceed to a point that is roughly in line with the seating that is already in place for the manuhiri. The group then stops and stands for a short time, in memory of the dead. All eyes are lowered. When going onto the marae, especially for a tangi, it is customary to "take a mate (deceased) with you". In other words, you recall a loved one, a family member, or a friend who has died.

Sometimes there will be a call from the tangata whenua indicating that the manuhiri have stood for long enough; sometimes there will be just a few spoken words with a gesture towards the seats or, perhaps, a final karanga inviting the manuhiri to come closer. At other times it is a matter of personal judgement as to what is an appropriate length of time. The group then sits. Its speakers and senior members, usually the menfolk, occupy the front seats. Older women, and those who will support the kai korero with waiata, sit close behind the speakers.

TE MARAE-ATEA / THE MEETING PLACE

In earlier times the complex of buildings and ground was termed the "pa" or "kainga". The term "marae" applied at that time only to the open courtyard. It was across this space that hosts and visitors exchanged speeches of welcome. It was here, too, that ideas were exchanged and a range of current topics were discussed.

The manuhiri walk onto the marae as the kai whakautu replies to the karanga (call of welcome).

Today the term "marae" is generally used to describe the total complex, including the open courtyard area. However, many kaumatua are now using the terms "marae-atea" or "marae-areare" to distinguish between the marae complex and the open courtyard. In this book the term "marae-atea" will be used when referring to the open courtyard.

The function of the marae-atea has not changed with the passing of time. It is still used as it traditionally was – for welcoming guests, for exchanging speeches, and for expressing points of view. Across the marae-atea it is quite proper to hurl challenges; it is quite proper to attempt to denigrate others to one's own advantage. The battle with words is as important as the creation of peace through words. Nevertheless, it is across this same space that words of prayer are shared.

The physical delivery and stances adopted by the kai korero mean that speakers often move forwards, backwards or sideways, but never so far forward as to cross to the immediate presence of the manuhiri. The space is tapu and is sometimes termed Te Turanga-o-Tu-te-ihiihi (the standing place of Tu Matauenga, the God of War). At other times it is known as Te Turanga-o-Tane-i-te-wananga (the standing place of Tane Mahuta, God of Man).

This area governed by Tu Matauenga provides a situation where contrasting behaviours can be practised. Insults are a fair exchange across the marae-atea, but insults are not acceptable within the whare tipuna, where Rongomatane, God of Peace, holds sway. The principle behind removing one's shoes at the door of the whare is to leave the dust of Tu

Matauenga (God of War) outside and not to take this dust into the house of Rongo (God of Peace). Thus, if slippers are worn inside the whare, these should not be worn outside. Whether slippers or shoes are worn outside is immaterial to the dust that is picked up and to the concept of that dust being of Tu Matauenga.

People who wear slippers inside the whare do not sit or walk on the mattresses with their slippers on. They sit on the mattress in such a way that their feet and their slippers are on the floor. If they choose to sit on the mattress and lean against the wall, then their slippers are removed from their feet and left at the edge of the mattress.

NGA MIHI, NGA WHAI KORERO / GREETINGS AND SPEECHES

On nearly all marae the tangata whenua usually speak both first and last. However, there are variations.

There are two main forms of mihi exchange on the marae-atea. The pattern used depends on the tribal affiliation of the tangata whenua.

The first pattern is termed paeke. In this all speakers on the paepae (those seats upon which tangata whenua speakers sit) speak first. Paepae refers both to the people chosen to sit in this particular place and to the seats themselves. Reference in speeches is made to the paepae tapu as a unit. There are at least two speakers, possibly more, and one immediately follows the other. When all have completed their speeches, the speakers for the manuhiri follow successively. Each speech is followed by a waiata. Ngati Whatua and the other northern tribes are among those who follow the paeke kawa.

The second pattern is described as "tu mai, tu atu". Here one of the tangata whenua speaks first and is followed by the waiata of embellishment. A manuhiri speaker then stands and replies. His speech is supported by a waiata. Speakers then alternate from tangata whenua to manuhiri to tangata whenua to manuhiri. The tribes of the Waikato federation are among those who follow this kawa.

With the tu mai, tu atu pattern, it is possible that the number of speakers from one group will outnumber those from the other group. Previously, it was considered a slight to the mana of the marae or the visitors if it was not possible to match speaker for speaker. However, the situation has changed somewhat. Where there are more manuhiri than tangata whenua speakers, the first speakers alternate initially but the second or third host speaker may, having noted the number of important persons among the visitors, offer to them the mauri (life essence) of the marae, giving them the right to speak successively.

The final speaker for the tangata whenua, as the last speaker in the exchange, then recovers the mauri.

The first speaker from the tangata whenua sometimes helps – not always in a subtle manner – in the selection of the manuhiri who will be expected to speak, by greeting specific individuals by name. The persons named risk insulting the tangata whenua if they do not stand and acknowledge the special welcome to them.

Across the marae-atea a
speech of welcome is given.

A speaker for the manuhiri
stands to reply.

In another rare situation tangata whenua may refer to an individual and indicate to that person that on this occasion, they would prefer him or her not to speak.

Conduct during this period should be dignified. When a large group of visitors is involved, and some speakers go on for a long time, others may get restless. People in close proximity to the marae-atea may talk quietly among themselves, although this is not encouraged. One is expected to take notice of what is being said by the speakers. Smoking is considered by most elders to be in bad taste, so it is best to refrain. Likewise, all should refrain from walking about in the immediate area of the marae-atea during the mihi. One must never walk in front of a speaker. If children are present, they too must be restrained from walking across the marae-atea at this time.

Some appropriate greetings

The following greetings are appropriate for use on the marae. They follow a particular format but need not all be used.

A tauparapara (awakening) drawing attention to the speaker:

Ka tangi te titi,	The mutton bird calls,
Ka tangi te kaka,	The parrot cries,

Ka tangi hoki ahau,
Tihei mauriora.

And I, too, call out,
Behold, the breath of life.

Or an alternative:

Korihi te manu,
Takiri mai te ata,
Ka ao, ka ao, ka awatea;
Tihei mauriora.

The birds begin to sing,
The morning breaks,
It's dawn, it's light, it's broad daylight;
Listen, I speak to you.

A mihi to the marae, the house, and those present:

Te whare e tu nei,
Te marae e takoto nei,
Tena korua.
Nga hau e wha,
Nga iwi e tau nei,
Tena koutou katoa.

The house standing here,
The marae lying here,
Greetings to you both.
People of the four winds,
People gathered here,
Greetings to you all.

A mihi to the hunga mate (the dead):

Nga mate, nga aitua,	The dead and those being mourned,
O koutou, ara o matou,	Both yours and ours,
Ka tangihia e tatou i tenei wa.	We lament for them at this time.
Haere, haere, haere.	Farewell, farewell, farewell.
Te hunga ora,	The living,
Tena koutou katoa.	Greetings to you all.

Tangata whenua could use this kind of mihi:

E nga mana,	To the honoured,
E nga reo,	To the speakers,
E nga iwi o te motu,	To the people of the land,
Nau mai, haeremai,	Welcome, welcome,
Haeremai	Welcome
Ki runga o tenei marae.	To this marae.

Speakers from the manuhiri could use this:

Karanga mai, mihi mai	Thank you for your welcome
Aku rangatira, tena koutou,	My elders, greetings,
Tena koutou, tena koutou katoa.	Greetings, greetings to you all.

Reference would then be made to the take (reason) for gathering together:

Karanga mai i a matou	Call to us
E whai nei	Who seek
Nga taonga o nga tipuna.	The treasures of our ancestors.

The speech could be appropriately concluded, after the waiata has been sung, with:

E nga mana	To the honoured
E nga reo	To the speakers
Rau rangatira ma	To the respected people
Tena koutou, tena koutou,	Greetings, greetings,
Tena tatou katoa.	Greetings to us all.

It must be remembered that these are just some of the greetings that may be used in a whai korero situation. It should also be pointed out that in some tribal areas women would not farewell the dead, except as part of their karanga.

USE OF WAIATA

Almost invariably, each speech is followed by a waiata. The practice of singing a waiata is peculiar to the Maori and it is one aspect of the culture that is being encouraged and shared. Maori people increase their mana (self-esteem) if they are able to sing their traditional waiata. It is only on a marae that this valued custom can be practised openly.

The kawa of some hapu is that the women – the "songbirds" – will begin the waiata. It is they who will decide which waiata complements their speaker's words. Some kaumatua will not travel without a woman, for it is she who will select and help him with his waiata.

It is the act of singing the waiata that is important. The quality of the singing might enrich the event, but it is the act of supportive singing that has most significance.

Although the waiata that is sung traditionally reflects what the speaker has said, this is not essential. However, when the waiata is appropriate to what has been referred to in the whai korero, the mana of the group and the speaker is heightened.

Certain waiata should be sung only on particular occasions. Some are used only for a tangi and should not be sung in other situations. Others used at a tangi may be sung, for the whai korero always includes remembering those who have died. Popular songs should be avoided during a welcome onto a marae. The manuhiri would not normally sing a waiata that welcomes a group onto the marae, for they are not in a position to do so. Some waiata are "tribal" waiata and should only be sung by members of that tribe.

Many waiata are short, easy to learn, and appropriate for any occasion. If in doubt, a hymn is always acceptable. It is advisable to be prepared with more than one waiata, as the group's mana is not enhanced if it is placed in the position of having to repeat a waiata that has already been sung earlier by the tangata whenua.

The waiata is quite different from the action song. When standing to support in the singing of a waiata, stand beside or slightly behind the speaker – never in front of him. (The speaker should ensure that he is not standing in such a position that others are forced to stand in front of him.)

Some appropriate waiata

Ka pinea koe, e au   I will pierce you
Ki te pine o te aroha   With the shaft of love
Ki te pine e kore nei   With the shaft that never
E waikura e.   Will rust away.
(Appropriate for any occasion)

Hoki, hoki tonu mai,	Return, come back again,
Te wairua o te tau,	The spirit of my love,
Ki te awhi reinga	To a spiritual embrace
Ki tenei kiri e.	Of this bosom.

(Tangata whenua to manuhiri or for a tangi)

Maku ra pea,	It is I,
Maku ra pea	It is perhaps I who will
Maku koe e awhi e;	Embrace you and assist you;
Ki te ara, ara tupu,	In the pathway of your growth,
Maku koe e awhi e.	I will enfold you.

(Any occasion except a tangi)

E hara i te mea	Love is not only
No naianei te aroha;	A thing of today;
No nga tipuna	It has been passed down
Tuku iho, tuku iho.	From our ancestors.

(Any occasion)

Whakaria mai	Send forth the light
Tou ripeka ki au,	Of your cross to me,

Tiaho mai	Shine down
Ra roto i te po,	Through the darkness,
Ki kona au	There will I be
Titiro atu ai,	Watching and waiting,
Ora, mate,	In life and death,
Hei au koe noho ai.	Abide in me.

(May be sung on any occasion; tune, "How Great Thou Art")

Tutira mai nga iwi,	Stand forth, people,
Tatou, tatou e;	Let us unite;
Tutira mai nga iwi,	Come forth, people,
Tatou, tatou e.	Let us be one.
Whaia te maramatanga,	Seek for enlightenment,
Me te aroha,	And for love,
E nga iwi,	All people,
Kia tapa tahi,	Work together,
Kia kotahi ra,	Unite together,
Tatou, tatou e	Let us be one.

(May be sung for informal occasions)

Tukituki ake nei
Te manawa e,
Mou e koe e hine (koro),
Kua wehea nei,
Me he oti pea
I tou tinana e
Hei piriti
Ki te rangi e.
(More appropriate for a tangi)

Sobs within me
My emotions,
For you our dear one,
Who has left us,
If it were possible
Your body
Would be a link
With the heavens.

THE HONOUR OF WHAI KORERO

When Pakeha groups visit the marae, the tangata whenua may ask visitors not to use English during the whai korero exchange on the marae-atea. English is permissible on every other occasion, but many Maori people wish to retain the use of their own language in this one situation. Maori speakers among the manuhiri should respond to this request to honour the marae-atea by standing and replying in Maori, though it might have been their intention to allow their Pakeha friends to speak.

Such requests are sometimes interpreted as the height of rudeness by those who can speak only English. This is certainly not the intention. Part of the spiritual depth of Maoritanga is expressed in the marae-atea whai korero. Many expressions, ideas and emotions can be conveyed by Maori people much more easily in their own language than in English. Another factor is that many of those who speak on the marea-atea are native speakers of Maori who feel uncomfortable and inadequate when using English. To them, speaking on the marae-atea is deeply significant, and they feel a responsibility to themselves, their people, and their marae to speak to the best of their ability.

Within the Maori world, where a father has three or four sons, the fourth son may not get an opportunity to stand on the home marae until he is quite old. The practice of the father speaking "on behalf of" gives very limited opportunities for the youngest to speak. Being invited to speak on the marae-atea is, therefore, a very high honour. The Maori speaker must earn the right over a period of time. Such a speaker is accorded the status of an orator: a special person able to speak on behalf of his people – those of the present, as well as those of past generations.

Certain situations might lead to a person declining an opportunity to speak. The first situation involves that of a younger person speaking ahead of a kaumatua. This could be accidental or it could occur when different groups arrive at the same time. A younger speaker, representing the first group, might have stood to speak for his group. The mana of the kaumatua in the second party might be thought to be slighted if he followed the ranga-tahi (youth).

In recent years an elder was selected by a Minister of the Crown to accompany him to

The kai korero (speaker) delivers his oration, his group behind him in support.

A waiata in the form of an action song is performed to support the kai korero.

different hui. The response by tangata whenua, because of the presence of the Minister, was to call on elders with mana to participate in whai korero and mihi. On one occasion a young person travelling with the kaumatua in the ministerial party stood and replied to a kaumatua welcome. The interpretation of this action was simply that, if the Minister wished to pass his mana to the "boy", it was his affair. However, other prominent persons among the manuhiri were not prepared to have a "youngster" speak for them and did not stand in reply to the tangata whenua mihi. In the same way, kaumatua among the tangata whenua indicated that, had they been aware that a "boy" was considered good enough to respond to them, they would not have taken part in the welcome. Instead, they too would have placed a "youngster" on the paepae to equate with the "youngster" of the manuhiri. Although this might have been seen as an insult to the Minister, the implications of a boy speaker seeing himself as equal to a kaumatua should have been understood by those concerned.

A second situation arises where women have attained positions of authority and status within the Pakeha system. They may be school principals, board chairpersons, mayors, or other dignitaries. As a part of their normal work, they may be responsible for welcomes to others. Some Maori men, deeply aware of their tribal tikanga, will refuse to speak if a woman has spoken before them, either as tangata whenua or as manuhiri.

Similarly, women of status in the Pakeha world can, and do, claim quite correctly the right to welcome people as part of a powhiri ceremony that they have organised in a Western-type building. Such situations require a great deal of shared sensitivity by all participants. Some

Maori people say that, if Pakeha people wish to use Maori protocol on particular occasions, then they should defer to the Maori rules that govern this type of protocol. On this basis, because women do not generally speak on the marae-atea, they should not welcome visitors as part of the powhiri occasion. Conversely, because women are usually entitled to speak in the whare, and the powhiri is taking place in a building, it could be reasoned with equal validity that they do have the right to speak on these occasions.

It can be argued that a woman who is a principal, mayor, president or manager, has the right to determine how her "marae" operates. She, and her "family", can determine the protocol that her "marae" adopts.

Nevertheless, there exists the possibility of an unexpected outcome. After an undoubtedly sincere welcome, her visitors do have the right to decline to reply. The situation is one of cultural conflict. Because the woman has spoken, she may have offended her guests – not by what she has said, but her action of speaking. Likewise, because the guests now choose not to respond, they may offend the host.

One way of resolving this issue is to ask the question, "Whose feelings are more important, mine – for I am the host – or theirs – for they are my guests?" Older Maori people will not willingly run the risk of offending their host or hostess. Rather than cause offence, they would choose to stay away.

The dilemma arises from a difference of cultural values. In the Pakeha context, one defers to the "office" of a person – such as a principal, a board chairperson, or a mayor. In the Maori context, the "person" is placed before the office that they hold. Tapu and mana are related to the person, not to any prestigious position that they may have.

As people continue to learn about one another, these situations remain sensitive ones. It could be that greater humility and understanding need to be shown by both parties in such exchanges, for both parties no doubt mean well.

Generally speaking, women do not have a speaking role on the marae-atea. Many of those who argue that women should have the right to speak on the marae-atea claim that this situation is one of female suppression. Such an interpretation might be upheld were the situation to be evaluated solely from the Pakeha perspective. Maori people, both men and women, see their involvement on the marae not only as a role but as a personal contribution to the identity of their people. By contributing to the whole tikanga, their own mana, and the mana of their marae, is uplifted.

A task is performed because it is necessary that it be done. All persons on the marae at a particular time are present because there is work to be done. Older Maori women on the marae are fully aware of their contribution to the building of the mana of the people, of the marae, and of the tribe. The whai korero on the marae-atea is but one part of the whole tikanga of welcome.

A further reason for the denial of whai korero to women on the marae-atea is that it is the place of Tu Matauenga, the God of War. It can be the place for abusive and warlike speech. The tapu of all women requires that they be protected from the possibility of abuse.

It is proper for the male orator to accept the risks inherent in representing his people before an unknown group. He becomes the potential target in a disagreement; he may receive abuse. The tapu of the woman demands that she not be presented as a target in this way.

Because the woman is tapu to the Maori, it is quite inappropriate to equate the role of women on the marae with what happens in today's society generally. The tapu accorded a woman on a marae acknowledges her "supremacy" over men. In extreme situations on the marae-atea a woman may demean a speaker; she has the "power" to terminate a man's speech. A woman who feels that someone has been speaking for long enough may, without censure, stand and begin his waiata. He then has no option but to finish speaking and join in the waiata. By deliberately crossing the marae-atea in front of a speaker, a woman can also terminate his speech. Such actions would be very rare, yet they are possible. The importance of the tapu as it applies to women is evidenced in the need for a puhi (a virgin) to participate in the opening of a whare.

Generalised statements that women are not allowed to speak on the marae-atea contain other errors. In addition to their responsibility for the karanga and waiata, women may speak on the marae-atea on special occasions, under exactly the same conditions as men. But they, too, must be accepted by their people as having the necessary mana to speak on behalf of others. This expectation applies also to Ngati Porou, a tribal area that accepts the right of women to stand and whai korero. There is no open invitation for either men or women to rise and speak in the whai korero part of the proceedings. The turangawaewae sanctions still apply. So, too, do the tapu sanctions and the expectation that a people's mana could be belittled by a poor speaker. Situations on marae outside Ngati Porou exist where women with mana, representing a group that is comprised wholly of women, have been given the right to speak on the marae-atea on behalf of their group. Such persons with a knowledge of Maori customs have generally done so after first moving to the whakamahau (porch) of the house. By so doing, they are protected by their ancestors who are represented in the house, and, with the knowledge of ancestral support, they speak from this position.

Some hapu groups in the city are beginning to find that the pool of menfolk able to take their place on the paepae is becoming smaller and smaller. Present economic circumstances now mean that people just cannot afford to take time off work, and there is the added risk of unemployment. As women themselves do not wish to trample on the tapu of their marae-atea, manuhiri are often given a karanga or powhiri and then taken inside the house, where the women mihi. This is an adaptation of marae kawa, but it is a modification created because of need. Nevertheless, the custom of only males speaking on the marae-atea has been retained and honoured. And, again, only those women who have the right to speak on behalf of the people will do so, even in this new situation.

Although some Pakeha and Maori people may see the absence of women in whai korero as a form of oppression, other Maori women who choose not to speak in these circumstances claim emphatically that they do not consider themselves oppressed in any way. They are quite adamant that their menfolk speak on their behalf, and they insist that the man says what the womenfolk want him to say. If the topic is a very important one, it will have been discussed many times by husband, wife and family. The responsibility of the speaker, then, is to express the consensus views of the family.

There are very few tribal groups that will not allow women to speak within the house. Yet, even so, when inside the whare (house), a Maori woman may choose not to speak if her husband, parents, brothers or elder sisters are present. This is because she believes that her speaking will demean their tapu. Similarly, some men will not speak after a woman has spoken. There is also the inherent belief that the tuakana (elder member of the family) has the right to speak on behalf of that family. This is especially so in the whai korero situation.

THE LAST SPEAKERS

The last speakers on the marae-atea have additional, special duties.

If there is a koha (gift) to be presented by the manuhiri, their last speaker will place the koha on the marae at the conclusion of his speech.

It is important that the last speech that occurs in the exchange – no matter how short – be made by a tangata whenua speaker. By doing so, the mauri (ethos) of the marae returns to the tangata whenua and is not carried away from the marae by the manuhiri on their return home.

TE KOHA / THE GIFT

The placing of the koha follows after the waiata used to tautoko (support) the speech of the last speaker for the manuhiri. This indicates to the tangata whenua that there will be no further speakers from the visiting group.

The koha should not be held in the hand during the speech. It is best left in a pocket until the correct time to place it on the marae.

The koha is placed on the ground in a position closer to the tangata whenua than to the manuhiri. This requires the last manuhiri speaker to cross the space that hitherto has not been crossed by either party.

The giving of a koha stems from the tradition of bringing gifts – usually of food – when visiting another marae. The manuhiri would bring foodstuffs that were plentiful in their area but in short supply in their hosts' district. For example, an ope (group) from inland Murupara, where birdlife might have been plentiful, would take preserved pigeons as their koha when visiting a marae at Whakatane on the coast. Tribal or hapu groups living near the coast would take dried fish or shellfish on visits to the inland areas.

In more recent times food that could be kept for long periods, such as kumara or smoked eels, has replaced the traditional koha. Before the advent of the "koha in an envelope", the koha of food would be taken straight to the pataka, without having to cross the marae-atea.

The koha is placed on the
marae-atea by the last
manuhiri speaker.

Karanga after the koha

A woman from the tangata whenua may karanga the koha. When the karanga is finished, the koha is picked up by one of the men, who indicates his gratitude to the manuhiri for their gift.

It is because of this karanga that one should leave the placing of the koha until after the waiata. If the manuhiri sang their final waiata after the hosts' karanga, it could appear as though they were trying to retain the mauri of the marae. Moreover, if the tangata whenua left a koha lying on the marae for a lengthy period, it could almost appear as though they were not keen to accept the gift from their visitors.

In some areas, the karanga for the koha will be given, but the koha itself will not be picked up until after the last of the tangata whenua has spoken. This is because those people believe that in picking up the koha you are indicating that there will be no further speakers, just as in placing the koha the manuhiri are indicating that there will be no further speaker from their group. Reference will always be made to the koha, however, by any further speakers. On other marae the koha will be picked up by a woman, before the final speaker for the tangata whenua stands to speak.

TE TUTAKITANGA / THE PHYSICAL CONTACT

A spokesperson for the tangata whenua now invites visitors to cross to the paepae to hariru

The ceremonial tapu is lifted when tangata whenua and manuhiri make physical contact.

The hongi ends the formality of the ceremonial welcome.

and hongi. Sometimes this will be the person who has delivered the final mihi; sometimes it will be the person who picks up the koha.

This person will generally indicate with a gesture which way visitors should move – whether from left to right or vice versa. The general rule is to move from the group of speakers towards the door of the whare. Whether you hariru, hongi, kiss, or do all three depends entirely upon your feelings at the time. Should a visitor recognise a special friend or family member, it would be proper to rejoice at such a meeting or to mourn and tangi (shed tears), especially if this is the first meeting since the death of a family member.

The action of performing the hongi is associated with the hariru. The two participants shake hands, each using the right hand. At the same time the left hand of each may be placed upon the other person's near shoulder. The head is bent, the eyes are closed, and the noses are pressed.

For some tribes the nose is pressed twice, for others it is pressed once only. Invariably, the tangata whenua will indicate their own kawa by example. It is appropriate to say "tena koe" or "kia ora" as part of the greeting; a Maori will sometimes murmur softly as noses are pressed.

Some groups press each side of the nose, rather than use direct pressure on the point of the nose. This is akin to the Continental kiss on each cheek.

Among some of the older people, foreheads will touch during the hongi, and this will be deliberate. This practice is found also in some African and Asian countries; it indicates a sharing of thoughts leading to a sharing of emotions through the touching of noses, the

After the formal welcome it's time to get to know each other.

holding of hands, and even the forming of a common pool of tears that have fallen from the eyes.

If the relationship is a close one, both hands may be held during the hongi. Indeed, if feelings are particularly strong, they may be shown by the holding of both hands, the hongi, and a kiss amid wailing and tears.

A stranger to the hongi/hariru should not hariru with the right hand and use the left hand to grasp the other person's right elbow or right forearm. This could indicate a feeling of doubt or a lack of complete trust. There is no place for doubt or tentativeness in a gesture designed to express loving, caring and sharing.

The hariru and hongi — the physical contact between tangata whenua and manuhiri — remove the tapu that existed as the result of entering and meeting on the marae-atea. The people and the marae-atea have now become noa (free from tapu). The tapu sanctions associated with the whakaekenga (entry) to the marae are now removed, because the tikanga associated with the tapu has been correctly followed. The tapu has been lifted, and the manuhiri are now tangata whenua for the duration of their stay. This process is often referred to as whakatangata whenua.

TE WHAKANOA / THE LIFTING OF MANUHIRI TAPU

Visitors are now free to move on any part of the marae and to take part in the welcoming of other manuhiri. The process of whakatangata whenua has been completed. Those who entered as visitors or manuhiri have now become tangata whenua.

The visitor has become a part of the marae for the duration of his or her stay. He or she is no longer a waewae tapu or first-time visitor to that marae. This is significant, for on a subsequent visit the visitor could enter without the formality of a powhiri – especially if arriving alone or at a time inconvenient for a semi-formal tangata whenua welcome.

This should not be taken to mean that the visitor has become tangata whenua in its fullest sense. One can only become tangata whenua in this deeper sense after many visits and after an obvious acceptance by the tangata whenua that one is a worker for the marae. A visitor is not presented with a key to someone's house after the first visit.

It is likely to take years of sharing happy and sad times before someone will offer a friend such a key.

TE WHARE TIPUNA / THE ANCESTRAL HOUSE

Immediately adjacent to the marae-atea and facing the main entrance is the whare. The manuhiri have been facing it; the tangata whenua have drawn strength and inspiration from its presence. The whare is referred to in one or more of the following ways: whare tipuna or whare tupuna (ancestral house), whare whakairo (carved house), whare nui (large house), whare hui (meeting house), whare moe or whare puni (sleeping house), or whare runanga (council house). The building is usually sited – as in the past – facing the gateway, with the marae-atea between the house and the gateway.

In every case the whare is named, usually after an ancestor. The whare tipuna at Tuakau is called Nga Tai e Rua (the two tides of people). This name was agreed to by Princess Te Puea and Sir Apirana Ngata. It signifies the meeting place of the two tides of people, the Ngati Porou from the East Coast and those of the Waikato confederation, the Tainui tribes.

The whare is also designed to represent the ancestor in a symbolic way. Thus the tekoteko (carved figure) on the roof top in front represents the ancestor's head. The maihi (carved pieces from the tekoteko extending towards the ground) represent the arms of the ancestor, held out in welcome to visitors. The tahuhu or tahu (ridge pole), which runs down the centre of the whare from front to back, represents the backbone. The tahuhu is a very long and solid piece of wood, for when the backbone is strong the body is strong. The heke or wheke (rafters), reaching from the tahuhu to the poupou (carved figures) around the walls, represent the ribs of the ancestor.

The poupou usually represent ancestors from the tangata whenua and other tribes. A person with an understanding of whakapapa (genealogy) will identify the relationship between the tribal poupou and the tangata kainga (people from that marae).

The pou tokomanawa (uprights) – of which there may be two in the whare whakairo – support the tahuhu and represent the connection between Ranginui, the Sky Father, and Papatuanuku, the Earth Mother. The act of entering the house is interpreted symbolically as entering into the bosom of the ancestor.

The interaction of people on the marae-atea is quite different from that inside the house. Within the whare, Rongo, the God of Peace, reigns. It is in this atmosphere, under a cloak of peace, that people interact with one another and with the spirits of their ancestors. Although intense discussions may take place, decisions are always made in peace.

Just as the poupou around the walls of the whare represent tribal ancestors, so too do other forms in the whare whakairo. Patterned panels, no matter how they are constructed, represent various ancestral customs or facets of people's behaviour that are seen as being important and deserving of presentation.

Thus patterns of tukutuku work have names that are well known to all tribes. The poutama, patiki, purapura whetu, and roimata patterns appear in most whare whakairo.

There are also certain painted patterns or kowhaiwhai. These most often feature on the heke. If the tahuhu is not carved, it will probably carry a kowhaiwhai pattern. These kowhaiwhai are recognised by all tribal areas, but some may have particular significance in their own areas. For example, in the whare puni Paku-o-te-rangi, at Putiki marae in Wanganui, the kowhaiwhai patterns all represent forms of food.

A study of kowhaiwhai patterns shows an emphasis on the use of forms that represent growth: seeds, the uncurling of the young fern frond, young curled leaves, shoots and branches. A life line is often featured – a central line, without any break, that leads back to past generations and forward to future generations, and from which new stages of growth develop. On some very old whare developed during the time of Te Kooti (a Maori prophet), birds and native flowers are used on the heke.

Although many whare seem to be of similar shape, there are variations in the pitch of the roof. On the Whaikowhatu marae at Lake Rotoiti, the steeply pitched roof of the whare tipuna – Tarawhai – was deliberately designed to comply with the traditional Tu-tama-tane style of whare. This roof stands out above the fence around the marae. The latter is constructed of sharpened branches set into the ground, giving the effect of the pa palisade of old.

In some areas the welcome takes place inside the whare rather than on the marae-atea. This is not uncommon, especially in those areas where, during a tangi, the tupapaku lies within the house rather than on the whakamahau (porch) or in a separate shelter set up for the tupapaku and the paremate (family of the deceased). Sometimes, if it is raining or very cold in those tribal areas where tikanga would normally require the outside exchange, it may be agreed by the tangata whenua that manuhiri will be welcomed inside the whare.

The same mihi format applies in these situations as would apply were the mihi being extended on the marae-atea outside. In this case, the marae-atea becomes that space within the whare that is left between the tangata whenua paepae and the manuhiri.

The areas where manuhiri and tangata whenua should sit or sleep within the whare are part of marae kawa. Among most tribes, tangata whenua sit to the left of the tatau (doorway). Those who sit or sleep nearest the door are the most honoured people of the tangata whenua.

The manuhiri therefore move to the right of the door as they enter. Those with the

Parts of the whare tipuna

1. Marae
2. Tekoteko
3. Maihi
4. Raparapa
5. Amo
6. Paepae
7. Roro, mahau
8. Tatau
9. Pare
10. Whakawae
11. Matapihi
12. Tahuhu
13. Pou tahu
14. Pou tokomanawa
15. Pou tuarongo
16. Tuarongo
17. Pakitara

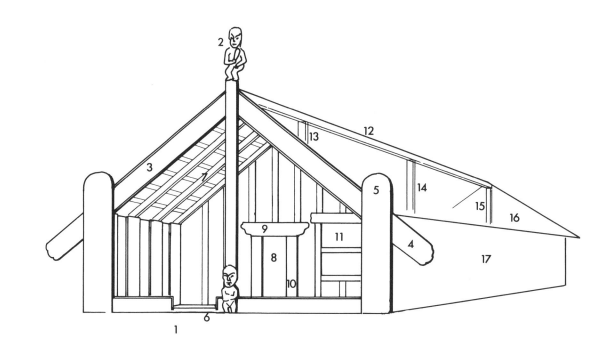

Inside the whare tipuna

A   Purapura-whetu
tukutuku
B   Poutama tukutuku
C   Patiki tukutuku
D   Poupou
E   Kaho
F   Heke
G   Kaho matapu

greatest mana are almost always expected to sit nearest the matapihi (window). But this does vary with certain tribes. The Te Arawa people, for example, expect their most respected manuhiri or kai korero to sit at the back of the whare, but still on the right-hand side. On Ngapuhi marae, where the welcome usually takes place inside the whare, the tangata whenua sit to the right of the tatau, under the window. The manuhiri sit at the back of the whare on their left-hand side facing the paepae or, alternatively, in the centre of the whare.

Almost invariably, on the back wall farthest from the door, in the place of greatest security and looking the full length of the whare, are photographs of those who have died. The number of photographs varies, and only occasionally are they named. Tangata whenua can identify these people, for the presence of their photographs indicates that they have played a prominent part in the life of the marae.

TE WHARE KAI / THE DINING ROOM

The whare kai or kauta (dining room) is the third essential part of the marae complex, the other two being the marae-atea and the whare tipuna. Its importance is emphasised in several whakatauki (proverbs):

Te tohu o te marae, ko te pataka.   Evidence of a good marae is the size of the pataka (food storehouse).

Kia tika mai a muri, ka nui te mana o mua.	If the back functions well, the front will gain prestige.

Years ago, when food preservation was achieved by salting or drying, a special structure called the pataka (food storehouse) was built.

The pataka is no longer found on marae. Hygienic food storage now involves refrigeration, and this is a part of present-day facilities. The table set for visitors is, however, still the final evidence of a good marae. No Maori wants his or her marae to gain a reputation for poor hospitality. There must be more than enough, so that manuhiri can always be asked, "Would you like more?"

Visitors, when thanking their hosts, frequently speak of the ringa wera – "hot hands" – in the kitchen. It is they who whakanui i te mana o te marae (increase the mana of the marae). The reputation of the marae and its rating in terms of hospitality are in the hands of the ringa wera – the cooks and the workers. No matter how eloquent and competent the speakers, if the person is not satisfied inside then the marae is rated poorly; it has failed to provide the expected level of hospitality.

Each marae has its own routines for setting tables and serving meals. Guests sit and are served their meal; very rarely, would there be a buffet meal for a large hui. Special catering arrangements are usually made for children. The tangata whenua and, of course, the ringa wera are fed last. Very good organisation is needed in order to cater for the large numbers

The ringa wera, working together preparing food, often discuss matters of concern.

of people attending a hui. There are often two or three hundred for one sitting. All must be fed, sometimes in three or more sittings. It is not correct to remain seated at the table, talking, when the meal is finished. When there are large numbers to be fed, the sooner one group leaves the table, the sooner another group can enter.

Each building has a specific role, and it is because of this role that each commands the respect of the people. Like the meeting house, the whare kai, too, is named. The ancestral name will have important associations for the people. For example, on the marae at Tuakau, the dining room is named Reitu. Reitu, a twin girl from Waikato, married a Northland chief, Ueoneone, and from this marriage there developed a strong link between Waikato and the Tai Tokerau tribes of the far north. Reitu, the dining hall standing on the marae at Tuakau, makes a point of expressing a special welcome to the Northland tribes, as well as to others.

The dining room is usually sited to the side or the rear of the meeting house. Rarely would it be sited so as to open directly onto the marae-atea, but it is usually within sight of the marae-atea. An example is the dining room Rangimaikuku on the Waikohatu marae. This is sited to the right of the whare tipuna Tarawhai. A tangata whenua rangatira explains it in this way:

For Te Arawa, the left side of the marae is the tapu side, the right side is noa. Therefore everything tapu takes place on the left side. There are practical reasons for this also. The whare kai and the facilities are on the right; the tangata whenua can therefore go on with their work on the marae without interfering with the tapu of the powhiri and the mihi.

The whare kai, then, is not a building in isolation. It is an essential part of the marae complex; it is the bearer of a name significant to the people; and, while fulfilling its essential marae function, it is identified with respect as part of the marae unit.

In more recent times, however, where land is at a premium on urban marae, the meeting house, dining room and ablution block have often been built as a single complex.

Kei te karanga te whare kai / The dining room calls

Visitors are now invited into the whare kai for a meal. When this call comes, the manuhiri speakers are expected to lead the way, supported by the kuia, who, in the past, would have entered the whare kai while rendering a happy waiata. Visitors must always consider their hosts. They should move into meals quickly, but without rushing. Hot food should be eaten when hot so that the meal is enjoyed at its best. Visitors may then comment favourably on the meal. Such comments mean a sharing in the whakanui i te mana o te marae.

A common area of concern to the ringa wera and those serving meals is that people often spread themselves along the tables, saving places for friends with whom they wish to speak. This is not helpful, as sufficient places are always set for all to be seated. In Maoridom, all people are important. So the person who is seated alongside you is as important as any friend you may have. Make sure, then, that all places at a table are taken before sitting at another table. It is usually best to fill a table from one end. By so doing, people are not left wondering where to sit.

The visit to the marae offers the opportunity to be with and to learn from other people.

Discussions during meals present an opportunity to make new friends. The whole concept of a marae hui includes the belief that all people are important. You express this philosophy by accepting that the person sitting next to you is an honoured person. To move somewhere else or to reserve a seat alongside you is to reject another person.

Another important courtesy concerns those who wish, often from habit, to sit talking at the table after a meal while others are trying to clear up around them. This unintentional nuisance arises from different cultural practices and habits. Pakeha people tend to sit and linger over a cup of tea, regarding it as a time for informal discussion. The marae people prefer to get the meal cleared away as quickly as possible, without rudely taking away food that is still required. Remember that the ringa wera do not eat until all manuhiri have been fed and the dishes washed and dried. Only then will they sit down to their meal. This happens even if there are two or three sittings, as required for a big hui.

Finally, remember never to sit on the tables at any time – in the kitchen, in the dining room, or in any other room. The reason is that people eat off tables; food is placed on tables. It is an insult to put one's posterior on a surface where, at some time, food will be served or prepared.

Whakapaingia nga kai / The blessing of the food

Always wait for grace to be said before commencing to eat. Grace is the blessing of the food on behalf of all present. Grace will always be said, and it will happen when a man from the tangata whenua draws attention to himself by banging on the table with a spoon, a knife, or his hand to obtain silence.

If you are among the first into the whare kai and, after a reasonable period of waiting, no one has said grace, stand and ask one of the host people whether they would like you to do so. If they accept, stand up, draw attention to yourself, and proceed with the grace. The main problem is timing. The ringa wera are keen that food should be eaten while it is hot. But the room should be reasonably full so that grace is said on behalf of all who are about to eat.

A further complication is that many visitors do not say grace in their own homes. They will therefore sit and begin to eat, and others around them will follow. All parties can be saved embarrassment if one remembers that food should always be blessed.

Some simple graces:

Whakapaingia enei kai
Hei oranga mo o matou tinana
Ko Ihu Karaiti hoki
To matou kai-whakaora
Amine.

Bless this food
To our use
For Christ is
Our Saviour
Amen.

Ringa wera in an open-air kitchen.

E te Karaiti,	O Lord,
Whakapaingia enei kai	Bless this food
Hei oranga mo o matou tinana,	For the sustenance of our bodies,
Whangaia o matou wairua	Feed our souls
Ki te taro o te ora,	With Thy spiritual food,
Nau hoki nga mea katoa	For all things are from You
Amine.	Amen.

Nga ringa wera / The workers

The ringa wera are part of the marae; they are therefore participants in the hui. They, too, will wish to join in karakia (prayers) and to participate in discussions wherever possible. Discussions that are seen as important to manuhiri are equally important to the ringa wera.

Some marae are happy for manuhiri to help with dishes after their first meal. The protocol for the first meal is that you, the manuhiri, are still very much guests. Once the first meal has been shared, then an offer to help with dishes, prepare vegetables, or set and clear tables is in order. Such an offer will be particularly acceptable when tangata whenua numbers are small.

Remember that in helping the ringa wera you are not instructing them. A marae will generally set a certain number of places at each table. They will have a certain number of

The hangi is lifted.

sets of butter, sugar and condiments per table. Some marae will wash dishes at one sink and prepare vegetables at another. It helps to watch what is happening before offering to help. Be prepared to be told what to do, because after years of experience the marae has found a way that suits its workers best. Don't be offended if a suggestion is made. Watch and do as suggested next time. Do not ask, "May I help?" Pick up a tea towel and join those drying dishes; pick up a knife and peel the vegetables. You, the visitor, sincerely wish to help. They, the ringa wera, want you to feel at home.

TE WHARE MOE / THE HOUSE FOR SLEEPING

Most marae sanctions are based on the recognition that marae property is the property of the people. It is there to be shared by all. Nothing is "mine"; everything is "ours". The resources and facilities are owned jointly. They need to be available and in good repair at short notice.

As with other parts of the marae, certain conventions apply to the whare moe. Unless specifically asked to do so, do not take your bedding into the whare moe before the first meal after your arrival. This is done after the meal.

The uninformed may have the impression that within the house it is "free and easy" and that visitors may "grab the first bed" – thinking, "I'll get my gear in first, so that I can sleep by the door". Traditionally, the area by the door is reserved for the most respected manuhiri and the senior tangata whenua. On entering the whare moe and seeking a bed, visitors should therefore leave the first three or four mattresses on both sides nearest the door vacant. Visitors rushing in to get the best places should remember that some people are identified by the tangata whenua as having special mana. Places of honour will be reserved for them in the house – by the door and below the window.

As with seating arrangements in the whare, the manuhiri will generally sleep to the right of the tatau (door), while the tangata whenua will sleep to the left. If there is a large group of manuhiri, only a few tangata whenua will sleep in the whare moe.

It is interesting to note that a whare moe that can accommodate a hundred Maori people comfortably is often considered too small for fifty Pakeha men, women and children. Tangata whenua wonder why a husband and wife, who share a bed in their own home, sometimes seem reluctant to sleep close together on a marae. Usually a marae will arrange bedding so that one pillow is placed at the head of a space that is considered sufficient for one person to sleep in – not necessarily one whole mattress. Remember that the whare is sometimes referred to as Tane Whakapiripiri – Tane who draws people closer together.

There is certainly no fear of falling off the bed. And do not be embarrassed if you snore – you will be in good company. Some people once recorded an "interview" with their sleeping friend. His responses were quite hilarious when replayed to him the next morning. The marae isn't all serious.

Sometimes an article will be put on a mattress or pillow to indicate that the sleeping place is occupied, but in terms of tikanga Maori there is no need to "stake a claim". It would be especially bad form to shift someone else's article and replace it with your own personal gear.

Spare pillows must not be moved from where they have been set out. Late arrivals need to know where the available spaces are. A pillow with no clothing or blanket under or on top of it indicates that the space is still vacant. A coat or sleeping bag place across a certain number of pillows usually means that these spaces are reserved for particular people. Should you have spare spaces on either side of your chosen mattress and two people or a family come looking for beds, be prepared to move along one, in order to allow them to be together. This is especially important with children. In a crowded house do not expect to have two pillows. Likewise, do not show a disinclination to share part of another person's mattress. If there appear to be spare mattresses, do not double them up to make a more comfortable bed. Mattresses in the house today are very similar to those in most homes.

Mattresses are for sleeping or sitting on. If it is necessary to move from one place to another in the whare, walk in the area between the rows of mattresses. Children should always be stopped from jumping, running or walking on or over mattresses and pillows. Occasions do arise when children of tangata whenua and manuhiri need to be corrected. They are sometimes tempted to pick up pillows and "fight" with them. Within the concept of whanaungatanga (extended family), each adult is the "parent" of all the children on the marae. Therefore they have the right and duty to prevent young people from showing disrespect for other people's property. Rarely will Maori parents smack their children in the whare. However, they frequently correct them and insist on proper behaviour.

Pillows are made for people to rest their heads on. They are not to be sat upon. The head, which is tapu, should not have to be placed on a pillow where others have thoughtlessly placed their kumu (backside). The habit of not sitting on pillows is taught in Maori homes and reinforced on the marae by the example of adults.

Suitcases or carry-alls should be left at the foot of the chosen sleeping space. They should be placed as tidily as possible so that there is room for others to move into or out of their bed space. The space between rows of mattresses is the passageway for all. A suitcase should not be left on the bed, for when korero (discussions) take place other visitors will also sit on the mattresses. It is a simple courtesy for occupiers to invite visitors attending the hui for a short time to share the mattresses when discussions are going on.

Maori people who go to a hui intending to stay overnight do not usually sleep in their day wear; they change into night attire. It seems that many of the younger generation have no qualms about dressing or undressing in public. In fact, this is frowned upon in the whare moe. It would be most unusual for an older Maori person, male or female, to stand and undress openly in the whare. It is possible for both males and females to dress and undress under a blanket or in a way that does not draw attention to themselves. Others sharing the house take care not to stare at those who are performing this task.

On one occasion, when a "new" marae group were ready to retire, the womenfolk began

Shoes are removed and left at the door of the whare moe.

trooping out to the showers to undress for bed. For this action they were severely reprimanded by an elder, who told them clearly that before the existence of modern ablution buildings people dressed and undressed in the whare moe with complete dignity. They, he said, should learn to do likewise. It was wrong, he stated, to believe that everyone in the whare wished to watch them changing. He did not wish to do so, nor did he wish the same group to watch him.

In spite of this, changing in the shower rooms is quite common today and equally correct. Tangata whenua do not wish to embarrass manuhiri or to make them feel uncomfortable.

The brushing of hair in the whare moe is acceptable, provided that hair from the head or the hairbrush does not find its way onto others in the process. This is an important caution for young girls with long hair. When hair is removed from a brush or comb, it should not be dropped onto the floor or bedding. It should be taken home and disposed of. The head of a person is tapu. As in other cultures, the hair may be used to makutu (bewitch) a person.

In some marae smoking is permitted in the whare. This is usually indicated to visitors by the presence of ashtrays or tins. People who wish to smoke are expected to sit at the edge of the mattress close to the passageway. One should not take the ashtrays onto the mattresses. Nevertheless, despite the presence of ashtrays, it is best to wait and see whether or not the local people smoke in the whare. The safest and most considerate action is to go outside to smoke when there is a break between speakers. However, a long wait outside in the cold may follow before there is another convenient break to enable one to return. Sadly, some marae now find it necessary to display "No Smoking" signs on the beautiful tukutuku panels within the whare moe.

If staying more than one night on the marae, blankets and clothes must be tidied before breakfast or before the early morning walk.

Clothing should not be hung on walls unless special pegs have been provided. In such cases the pegs above the sleeping space belong to the sleeper. It is a matter of courtesy to leave pegs available for others rather than hang individual garments on separate pegs.

On the last day at the marae, personal gear should be removed from the house after breakfast, unless the tangata whenua suggest that the visitors wait until after the hui whakamutunga (the last session with the group together) or the poroporoaki (farewells and blessing). Being in a hurry to remove your gear implies that you can't wait to get away from the marae and that your stay has not been a very happy one.

KARAKIA / PRAYERS

Most marae have karakia – an acknowledgement of a spiritual presence – in both the early evening and the early morning. A short karakia often precedes or concludes the whai korero. These services are usually brief and are not aligned to any particular denomination. When there are a number of ministers of different denominations present, they will usually share parts of the service. If a service begins when people are in night attire and there is a need to stand, it is perfectly in order to stand either in a sleeping bag or with a blanket wrap. Marae practice is to stand for the singing of a hymn, unless the minister signifies to all that they may remain seated. It is not correct to lie down during karakia – you should sit up with your back to the wall.

TE TAKE / THE REASON FOR GATHERING

Now that the group is assembled, what is it here for? Every hui has a take – a reason for people coming together. Whether it is to discuss a single issue or a number of matters in a weekend seminar, the kaupapa (format) that the hui will take will be set out, usually by a kaumatua or someone from the paepae.

Sometimes the discussion will take place on the marae-atea, but most often it will be in the whare. People will sit on the mattresses and the paepae will sit just inside the door, sometimes to the left, but most often in front of the window. They will sit on seats, from which they will direct the hui. The paepae can be the kaumatua, the hui organisers, or the speakers. On some marae the tangata whenua kaumatua will maintain the paepae until after the first karakia; then they will hand the paepae over to the hui and its organisers.

On the marae-atea only those who have been selected to speak will do so on behalf of the group. Inside the whare, however, discussions will take place under the mantle provided by Rongo (God of Peace), so that all may speak, unless some feel strongly that only the older or male members of the family should speak for them. On most occasions women will be permitted to speak. If one is not sure whether or not the marae encourages women to speak, a male member of the group may ask the paepae.

Inside the whare, though discussion may be frank and sometimes heated, it is always conducted in peace. Quite often during heated debate people will be heard to say, "Kia tau te rangimarie" ("Let us be peaceful").

When speaking in the whare, it is usual to stand. There are exceptions, especially with Te Arawa women, who will normally not speak but if they do wish to express their views will remain in a position that does not elevate them above their menfolk or elders.

The whai korero format can apply when speaking for the first time at a particular hui. The speaker will first draw attention to himself by saying:

Or	Tena koutou.	Greetings to you all.
	Tihei mauriora.	(I issue) the sneeze of life.

One could then follow the normal whai korero format. You greet the house:

Te whare e tu nei,	The house that stands here,
Tena koe.	I greet you.

Speaking inside the whare nui.

Speaking in the whare tupuna. By standing near the wall, the speaker can turn and address all areas of the house.

Then the marae:

| Te marae kei waho, | The marae outside, |
| Tena koe. | I greet you. |

Then, because the house and the marae represent the elements that provide for people, you may greet them both:

| Te whare, te marae | The house and the marae |
| Tena korua, tena korua. | Greetings to you both. |

You may then recognise the spiritual presence that is always there:

| Nga mate | The dead |
| Haere, haere, haere. | Farewell, farewell, farewell. |

One must then return to the living with a greeting:

Tatou te hunga ora	To us the living
Tena koutou, tena koutou,	Greetings, greetings,
Tena tatou katoa.	Greetings to us all.

Then you may discuss whatever the topic is.

Perhaps the most important aspect of a marae hui is that people have the right to be heard and others have an obligation to allow them to speak without interjections or interruptions. A speaker should be allowed to say his or her piece without opposition and without heckling. If you disagree with what the speaker is saying, go to sleep or await your turn in the knowledge that you will also be extended the same courtesy.

People are not specifically invited to express their points of view – all automatically have that right. Rarely is there a chairperson, though the paepae will control a hui if they feel the need to do so.

During a discussion it is considered ill-mannered to walk in and out of the whare, especially if this means walking between the paepae and the person who is speaking. If possible, wait until a speaker is about to sit down before leaving the whare. This applies also when you want to enter the whare. It is possible to enter during a speech, providing you create as little disturbance as possible. It is best to sit just inside the door, moving to your place further inside when the speaker has finished speaking.

POROPOROAKI / FAREWELLS

The poroporoaki or speech of farewell is as important as the powhiri and speeches of welcome. It is the "letter of thanks" that is delivered in a face-to-face situation between the tangata whenua and their visitors.

If you are with a group that will be leaving at a set time, some time will be set aside for the poroporoaki. This will be after the hui whakamutunga or immediately after the hakari (final feast). If it is necesssary for one or more individuals – especially well-known people – to leave before the hui ends, it would be appropriate for their poroporoaki to take place during the last meal at which the person or group is present.

In all cases the poroporoaki is begun by the manuhiri. All those who wish to speak will do so consecutively. It is their opportunity to express their thanks and gratitude to the tangata whenua and, more especially, to the ringa wera. Here, again, speeches could be embellished by waiata, generally waiata that are lighter and happier than those for the powhiri. This is an opportunity for groups to use waiata-a-ringa (action songs) to show their appreciation. If a koha is to be left, this is given, once again, by the last speaker from the manuhiri.

The tangata whenua then speak, having decided just how long the manuhiri will be detained. On one occasion a well-respected person wished to leave a hui early to attend a rugby match and revealed this during his poroporoaki. The tangata whenua, however, did not wish him to leave, so they physically closed and spiritually locked the door of the whare. During lengthy speeches from a number of speakers, he was detained in the house for a further hour. This was done and taken with good humour, but stresses that people, not time, dictate what happens on the marae.

At the poroporoaki for the main group the tangata whenua conclude with karakia. The manuhiri are then free to leave after they have had a final hariru with their hosts.

A SUMMARY OF POINTS TO REMEMBER

- A marae is not a public park – it is the home of a group of people.
- Tangata whenua will make you welcome but will expect you to follow the kawa of the marae.
- You will be able to contribute towards the koha.
- Leave your blankets and personal gear outside until the welcome is concluded.
- Go onto the marae in silence – remember that it is a gathering of the living and the dead.
- Sit in the front row if you are a speaker; otherwise occupy the rear seats.
- The marae-atea is tapu throughout the welcoming ceremony.
- On some occasions the Maori language only is used during whai korero.
- Do not walk about while speeches are in progress, and never walk directly in front of a speaker. Children are welcome but should be reasonably quiet during the speeches.
- Attitudes to women speaking on the marae vary, so local kawa should be followed.
- In the whai korero exchange the last speaker should be from the tangata whenua.
- In the physical contact between the hosts and guests, you may hariru, hongi or kiss, as you choose.
- At the conclusion of the welcome the marae-atea ceases to be tapu and becomes noa.
- Shoes are removed before entering the whare nui.
- Certain places in the whare nui are reserved for the seating or sleeping of kaumatua.

- In the whare kai do not keep places for friends.
- Wait for grace to be said before starting your meal.
- Leave the whare kai as soon as you have finished your meal – others may be waiting to eat.
- After the first meal, be prepared to help the ringa wera in the preparation of food or with washing dishes.
- Never sit on a table.
- Do not sit on pillows in the whare moe.
- You may dress or undress discreetly in the whare moe.
- Refrain from smoking in all whare unless express permission is given.
- Do not use cameras or tape recorders unless prior permission has been obtained.
- Be prepared to say a few words of greeting in Maori in the whare hui and of farewell at the poroporoaki.

Te whare karakia

THE CHURCH

Often sited on or near a marae is a church building. Its presence symbolises the arrival of Christianity. The Maori has always worshipped on the marae-atea, in the whare tipuna, at the urupa, by a tree, on a hill, beside a river, or wherever and whenever there seemed to be a need. But after the arrival of Te Rongopai (Christianity) churches appeared. These places, the Maori was told, were the right places to worship; God lived in these places, and if God was to listen to prayer, it was necessary to go to church to pray.

Even if the church is associated with a particular faith, in Maoridom it is used for services by all denominations. The congregation attends services at the church irrespective of the affiliation of the minister.

The church may be carved or contain carved work – perhaps the pulpit, the doors, or the communion rail. There are often kowhaiwhai and tukutuku panelling. At least part of the service in these churches is conducted in the Maori language.

When hui are being held on the marae, though most spiritual ceremonies are conducted in the whare tipuna, there is usually an occasion set aside when all on the marae can share one service in the whare karakia.

All parts of the marae thus have a shared use – the marae-atea, the whare tipuna, the whare kai, and the whare karakia. This association is further emphasised by the naming of the church, which is usually after an ancestor of the tangata whenua or after a person who has played an important role in the lives of the tangata whenua.

Visitors address the whare karakia directly and recall that those who have contributed to life in the past, though now dead, remain a part of life.

Some appropriate hymns

Tama ngakau marie	*Son of peace*
Tama ngakau marie	Son of Peace
Tama a Te Atua	Son of God
Tenei tonu matou	Here are we always
Arohaina mai	Shown compassion.
Murua ra nga hara	Wipe away our sins
Wetekina mai	Unshackle

Enei here kino
Whakararu nei.

Takahia ki raro
Tau e kino ai;
Kei pa kaha tonu
Ko nga mahi he.

Homai he aroha
Mou i mate nei.
Tenei ra, e Ihu
Takina e koe.

Tenei arahina
A tutuki noa
Puta i te pouri
Whiwhi hari nui.

These evil ties
That beset us.

Suppress
All that is harmful;
Lest evil deeds
Retain their force.

Give to us the love
For which you died.
At this time, O Lord
Be Thou our guide.

Lead us
Until life's end
Take us from life's darkness
Into Thy happiness

Ma te marie

Ma te marie a te Atua
Tatou katoa e tiaki
Mana ano e whakau
O tatou ngakau ki te pai.

Ma te Atua Tamaiti ra
Ma te Wairua Tapu hoki
Ratou Atua kotahi nei
Tatou katoa e whakapai.

Koutou katoa ra

Koutou katoa ra
Mea iti nei
Haere mai koutou kei whakaroa
Tenei a Ihu, nana te ki
Haere mai ra ki au.

Chorus

Nei te hari tino hari nui

The grace of God

By the grace of God
We will be protected
He will also make steadfast
Our hearts towards things that are good.

May the Son of God
And the Holy Spirit
God in one
Bless us all.

Come to the Saviour

Come to the Saviour
Make no delay
Here in His word He has shown us the way
Here in our midst He's standing today
Tenderly saying come.

Joyful, joyful, will the meeting be

A te wa e tutataki ai
Hui atu tatou ropu katoa
Runga te rangi nei.

Nei ra whakaaro tuturutia
Tana e ki nei, me whakaae
Nana te tono, nana te ki,
Haere mai ra ki au.

E te Ariki
E te Ariki
Whakarongo mai ra kia matou.
E te Ariki
Titiro mai ra kia matou
Tenei matou o tamariki
E whakapono ana matou
Ki a koe.
Aue, aue
Te Matua, te Tamaiti
Wairua Tapu e.

When from sin our hearts are pure and free
And we shall gather Saviour with Thee
In our eternal home.

Think once again He's with us today
Hear now His blest command and obey
Hear now His accent tenderly say,
Will you my children come.

The Lord
O Christ
Listen to us.
O Christ
Look at us
We are your children
We believe
In you.
Aue, aue
The Father, the Son
And the Holy Ghost.

Te Matua, te Tamaiti
Wairua Tapu e.

The Father, the Son
And the Holy Ghost.

E te Atua
(Tune: Amazing Grace)

E te Atua kua ruia nei
O purapura pai
Homai e koe he ngakau hou
Kia tupu ake ai.

O Lord who has spread
Your good seed
Give us a new heart and strength
And let it grow stronger.

E Ihu kaua e tukua
Kia whakangaromia
Me whakatupu ake ia
Kia kitea ai nga hua.

O Lord let it not
Be lost
But let it thrive so that
The results may be seen.

A ma te Wairua Tapu ra
Matou e tiaki
Kei hoki ki te mahi he
O matou ngakau hou.

Let the Holy Spirit
Guide us
Lest our hearts should
Return to evil deeds.

Hangu te po

Hangu te po
Tapu te po
Marino, marama
Ko te whaea
Me te tama
Tama tino tapu rawa
Moe mai i te marie
Moe mai i te marie.

Mo Maria

Mo Maria aianei
O tatou waiata
Kia kaha ra tatou
Kia nui te aroha.

Chorus

Mo Maria aianei
O tatou waiata
Kia kaha ra tatou
Kia nui te aroha.

Silent night

Silent night
Holy night
All is calm, all is bright
Round yon virgin
Mother and child
Holy infant, tender and mild
Sleep in heavenly peace
Sleep in heavenly peace.

To Mary

To the Blessed Virgin
We sing our prayers and praises
Give us strength
Fill us with love.

To the Blessed Virgin
We sing our prayers and praises
Give us strength
Fill us with love.

Aroha ki a Maria
Aroha ki te Atua
I te rangi te whenua
Ake tonu, ake tonu.

Sing praises to the Blessed Virgin
Sing praises to the Lord
Who has dominion over all
Eternally.

The Lord's Prayer and the Benediction

Inoi ki te Atua

E to matou Matua i te Rangi
Kia tapu tou ingoa
Kia tae mai tou Rangatiratanga
Kia meatia tou e pai ai
Ki runga i te whenua
Kia rite ano ki to te Rangi
Homai ki a matou aianei
He taro ma matou mo tenei ra
Murua o matou hara
Me matou hoki e muru nei
I o te hunga e hara ana

The Lord's Prayer

Our Father who art in Heaven
Hallowed be Thy name
Thy Kingdom come
Thy will be done
On earth
As it is in Heaven
Give us this day
Our daily bread
And forgive us our trespasses
As we forgive those
Who trespass

Ki a matou
Kaua hoki matou e kawea kia whakawaia
Engari whakaorangia matou
I te kino
Nou hoki te Rangatiratanga
Te kaha, me te kororia
Ake, tonu atu
Amine.

Against us
Lead us not into temptation
But deliver us
from evil
For Thine is the Kingdom
The power, and the glory
For ever and ever
Amen.

The Benediction

Kia tau ki a tatou katoa
Te atawhai o to tatou Ariki
Te aroha o te Atua
Me te whiwhingatahitanga
Ki te Wairua Tapu
Ake, tonu atu
Amine.

Descend upon us
The grace of our Lord Jesus Christ
The love of God
And the fellowship
Of the Holy Spirit
For evermore
Amen.

Te urupa

THE CEMETERY

Hine-nui-te-po will one day call to herself, without exception, each one who lives. Because this is so, and because the whanau (family) wish to care for the place where the bodies of their own are entrusted to the care of Mother Earth, an urupa is established in association with a marae.

Sometimes the urupa lies adjacent to the marae. Young Maori children often tease one another, or attempt to frighten one another, by reference to the kehua (ghosts): "Watch out or the kehua will get you." Yet, despite this deliberate attempt to create fear, these same children are taught that they need not fear the dead.

Families have always wished to return to the whanau or hapu urupa. It is as much the wish of the individual to return as it is the desire of the family to bring their dead "home". Older people will express the wish to be "taken home". Yet, because in marriage there is a link with another area, there exists for each person at least two "homes".

Most urupa are situated close to the marae. Where it is possible, these sites are on a hill, overlooking the sea, a river, or the marae. In these special tapu places – places of natural beauty – Papatuanuku cares for the bodies of her charges.

A visit to the urupa is important if one is returning home after a long absence. Here is a place where Mother Earth provides the last pillows upon which the heads of the departed may rest.

At the urupa members of families are usually reserved places within the family rows. As the family were together in life, so the family is together in death.

It is a place where a visit serves to reinforce knowledge of a personal whakapapa. It is possible to move from grave to grave among the members of the extended family. Visitors to the urupa should take time to reflect: to consider the significance of the urupa; to remember the deeds of different family members; to consider their own contribution to the world that has been entrusted to them by those named in stone or on wood; to sing a familiar waiata; to embrace all who are lying together; to sing quietly the favourite hymn of a departed relative. It is not enough to come just to change the flowers.

It is important that the tapu of the area be recognised by visitors. On leaving the urupa, its tapu is removed by washing the hands in water. Many urupa have containers of water placed just outside the gate for this purpose. Other urupa can be reached only by crossing a creek. It is here that visitors or family will stop to wash their hands.

In the absence of water, it may be that rewena (home-cooked bread) is available. Should this be so, then the bread is crumbled and used to "wash away" the tapu. This action recreates the state of noa or freedom to move among, and have contact with, others.

Tangi

FUNERALS

The tangi or tangihanga embraces the funeral rites accorded a person before the body is finally interred. The Maori belief is that the tupapaku should not be left on its own at any stage after death. Hence people will gather to take the tupapaku from the undertaker's premises to the marae or place where it will lie in the company of people until burial. Family and friends may come and go from this place as they wish or they may remain until after the actual burial.

All people, including relatives arriving for a tangi, will go through the usual karanga and mihi procedures.

The coffin is left open. People will touch the tupapaku. Speeches will be made directly to the tupapaku in the belief that the spirit does not leave the vicinity of the body until the burial. The acceptance of the physical body in life requires a similar acceptance in death.

Although, to some people, the constant shedding of tears may appear excessively traumatic, Maori people believe that this actually eases the loss that they bear. People often travel many hundreds of kilometres to attend the funeral of a friend or family member to show their respect for that person and to give their support to the immediate family.

These notes are extremely brief, but the tikanga expressed at a tangihanga reinforces the full range of values that identifies the Maori culture as "being Maori".

The importance of the marae for a tangi is, in part, the fulfilment of the wairua or spiritual being of the Maori – the belief that those who have died are always with the marae, that the recently dead are released into the care of the long dead. It is important to the Maori that the dead be brought together to be greeted, respected and farewelled.

It is equally important that the living come together to support each other. By supporting each other on the marae, the living are made aware of their place in life. They are also reminded of the role of those who have died and the manner in which they are affected by their spiritual presence.

Some people will remain at a tangi for a few hours; others will remain overnight or for two or three days. A marae has learned to cope with fluctuating and uncertain numbers of people.

Marena

WEDDINGS

Marae are still being used for Maori weddings, mixed-race marriages, and even, occasionally, the marriage of non-Maori couples.

Many marae will not allow the consumption of alcoholic liquor on the premises, including the whare kai. Even when it is permitted, only very limited quantities are acceptable for a special occasion like a marena.

In accordance with general marae procedures, specific invitations are not generally issued to a wedding. Instead, all are welcome. This can place considerable financial strain on the host family unless they have wide family support. The giving of a koha does not always automatically occur, as it does in other marae situations, for sometimes the koha may be in the form of a wedding gift to the bride and groom.

Usually, however, groups of visitors to the marae will receive the customary powhiri, and after the whai korero, the koha gift to assist the family will be placed on the marae.

An important consideration is that the marae may be needed at the last minute for a tangi. Tangi take precedence over all other marae uses. It is not unknown, however, for a wedding to take place while a tupapaku is lying on the marae. Although this may be unthinkable to the non-Maori, to the Maori there is nothing illogical about celebrating occasions related to the living and dying in the same place. This is a good example of Maori wairua – the belief that life and death are intimately intertwined. The belief that the spirit does not leave the vicinity of the body until burial means that the spirit of a loved parent or family member is present to witness the marriage; the deceased shares spiritually in the ongoing life of the living. On this occasion death is very much a part of life.

Such occasions are rare, but the focus remains on people. All emotions are shared at the same place on the same day by the same people. Sadness and joy cannot be separated from those who live.

Types of marae

Generally, three types of marae now exist.

HAPU MARAE

This type is used mainly by the direct descendants of the person who established it and some of the descendants who still reside in the vicinity. Members of the immediate family who live away from the area return mainly for tangi or weddings. The pressures of maintaining the fences, grounds and buildings on the few family members residing in the vicinity are quite heavy. A family marae maintains its own tikanga, carries its own mana, and provides the same systems of support that large marae provide.

IWI MARAE

This type is used by all in the district. In smaller rural communities all those who associate with the marae will take part in all of its activities. In the towns any person or group may host others and use it as their marae kainga (home marae). In such urban situations other members of the community, though living within easy reach of the marae, may not become involved. In the event of a tangi, however, all of the local people come together to assist in the hui.

Fund-raising for marae upkeep in this situation is usually a community effort, but members of the iwi (tribe) see this as their particular responsibility.

Many family members now live in the cities. These family may form marae committees in town to support the marae "back home". They raise funds for locally planned marae improvements and will often travel home for a tangi to support the bereaved. City dwellers frequently take their families home for holidays. Several families may live together on the marae at these times.

URBAN MARAE

Modern in design and rich in their range of Maori crafts, these are often set up by groups of people from particular tribal areas or by people of a particular religious order. The initial unity or bonding is either tribal or religious. However, such marae do serve the community at large and do not restrict their use to one tribal or religious group. They are easily able to cope with large visiting groups, since they have a large group of associated tangata whenua to call upon for assistance.

Urban church marae are based within and are a part of the church buildings, but in other respects they function as normal marae. Other religious groups, or any group for that matter, are welcome to use the facilities, even though such persons may prefer to use their own church marae if they have one.

SCHOOL MARAE

A number of schools, both urban and rural, have established whare hui in a marae setting within the school grounds. The marae is used for conventional purposes, such as welcomes and hui, and in addition can be the centre for the study of taha Maori and Maori language. Although some rural schools prefer their Maori pupils to identify with their own local marae, others establish school marae to give Pakeha pupils, as well as Maori pupils, the opportunity to participate in Maoritanga.

There is no doubt that many Maori youngsters who have lost contact with their own iwi marae find that they establish a close bond with their school marae.

There was initially some resistance in the community – from both Maoridom and the Pakeha sector – to the establishment of school marae, but it now appears to be generally accepted that this extension is a positive and worthwhile one.

OTHER MARAE

Today many people use the term "marae" for any area on which they choose to welcome visitors, especially when they choose to use a format corresponding to that of a marae welcome. A room, therefore, may loosely, though acceptably, be referred to as a marae for the purposes of welcoming visitors. Reference in the speech of welcome to Papatuanuku is likewise acceptable, for Mother Earth supports the foundations of every building.

Similarly, a hall may be referred to as a marae – providing there is first a karanga, usually at the entrance to the building, and the process of mihimihi (exchanges of greetings) is practised. In Te Araroa, for example, the lack of a local marae with marae-atea, whare tipuna, and whare kai has been overcome by the people making use of a local facility, the Awatere Memorial Hall. The stage serves as the sleeping quarters for small visiting groups.

Another example is that of an office being used by its staff as a marae when welcoming visitors. This happens quite regularly at the Office of the Race Relations Conciliator in Auckland. Again, the Auckland City Council used the Central Library as a marae to open its collection of rare New Zealand manuscripts.

By choosing to adopt the protocol of a Maori welcome and by being aware of its implications, the assembly hall, the staff room, the church hall, the school car park, or the town hall may be referred to as a marae. The important thing is that all such places belong to "us", not to "me". They are places where thoughts and ideas may be exchanged, and joy and sadness may be shared. All of these places need people in order to come alive. Within such places, wairua is not denied. Any place can become the marae, because any area of land can become the representative of Papatuanuku, the Earth Mother.

Despite such concessions, Maoridom is very much aware of the implications of turanga-waewae and of the Maori language. This is not because Maori is the only language known, or because it is the only one spoken in these situations, but because Maoridom is aware of the need for people – both Maori and non-Maori – to appreciate the joy of sharing.

The marae is a place of deep significance to those Maori people who have grown up knowing their marae or to those who, in later years, have responded to the desire to come to terms with their identity.

It needs to be reiterated that what has been written in this book is just the basic concept of what a marae is and what it means to the Maori people. There has been no attempt to cover every aspect or every variation of marae kawa. This cannot be done in a book such as this, for each iwi must be responsible for stating its own deeper marae philosophies and concepts. This book is just the beginning. Different people may take different paths to the same destination: a much greater identity with, and understanding of, our marae.

A marae is for people of all
ages to share.

Maori values and concepts

The Maori has a set of values and a philosophy of physical, procedural and human structures that reflect these values. The following explanations are necessarily brief and are intended only to give a very general picture.

AROHA

As an extension of manaakitanga (caring), aroha is the concept of love in its widest sense. It can mean respect, concern, hospitality, and the process of giving. Thus every person is concerned for, and respects, the rights of others. Aroha is given freely; it does not take account of personal cost but considers only what is beneficial to others.

Aroha is reflected in the way that the tangata whenua provide hospitality; in the way that the manuhiri become part of the tangata whenua and share in the normal duties of the day; and, more importantly, in the way that people relate to one another. The essential elements of interpersonal relationships involving aroha are respect, friendship and care.

The aroha of a person makes no demands on another. There are no conditions laid down before the giving of self. "I, in every way that you require, will serve you. In the same way that I must care for you, I must care for all."

HEI WHAKAMAHANA

This refers to feelings of warmth and welcome. Many believe that a marae without its kaumatua is cold. The presence of older people make a marae seem warm and comfortable. This is possible because the older people are unhurried; they give a feeling of serenity because they have time to sit and talk. For the Maori, there is the knowledge that the kaumatua know what to do at all times, and though they may direct and reprimand, by their presence and their actions they convey feelings of warmth, serenity and security.

Associated with many marae is a whare mahana. Most often it is occupied by an elder, his wife, and some mokopuna (grandchildren). The occupiers of the whare mahana have the duty and commitment, on behalf of their iwi, to make the marae a warm place to visit.

Unlike the Pakeha role associated with most "caretakers", the occupiers of the whare mahana "welcome people in"; they do not "chase them out". They keep the marae warm for visitors. They maintain the fires of aroha for all people who wish to visit the marae.

KAUMATUA AND KUIA (TAUA)

Kaumatua and kuia are elders and, as such, should be respected, cared for and acknowledged. They are respected for their life experience; they are respected for their knowledge; they are respected for their wise counsel. It is they who have been responsible for the maintenance of taha Maori.

There is no specific time or age at which a person automatically becomes a kaumatua. Rather, a whanau confers mana and the status of kaumatua upon an elder whom it wishes to regard in a special way. It sees in a kaumatua a person who is knowledgeable about tradition, wise and experienced; someone whom the whanau will wish to consult on aspects of Maoridom that seem to require an answer.

Thus kaumatua have an honoured place in the whanau. They are sometimes figuratively referred to as precious taonga of the marae, the hapu, or the iwi. They are precious people who have a very special place in the community.

KAWA

Kawa is Maori protocol. It varies between tribal groups, though basic principles are common to all. For instance, all manuhiri are welcomed with speeches and respond with speeches, but the format adopted in the welcome – whether by the paeke or the tu mai, tu atu format – depends upon the kawa of the tribe on whose marae the hui is being held. The important thing is that the kawa of the marae demands that people are welcomed and cared for throughout the hui.

There are other occasions when the kawa of a particular tribal group is followed. For example, the Auckland City Council, when introducing a Maori component into a ceremony, uses the Ngati Whatua or Wai-o-Hua kawa. That is, they use protocol that applies to the Ngati Whatua and the Wai-o-Hua people, who are the tangata whenua of the Auckland area.

Following the correct tikanga kawa or procedure indicates respect for the local people. The visitor has made a special effort to find out the correct protocol to follow in order not to cause hurt or embarrassment. By following such a protocol, he or she is freed from the tapu prohibitions of the marae.

MANA

Mana is usually translated as "status" or "prestige", though these words are inadequate. Neither indicates the degree of humility that is associated with mana.

Mana may be acquired by simply being the senior member of the family. This is the mana that kaumatua have to whai korero and that kuia have to karanga.

The mana that gives some people the ability to deal with psychic matters is also passed down genealogically. This is usually handed down by an ancestor to one who has been specially schooled in these matters.

Some people outside the normal lines of inheritance can also be given mana because of certain gifts or talents that they have. These people are not always in the public eye; they may be quiet workers in the background.

People who work for the mana of their marae do not necessarily acquire mana for themselves as individuals. Although members of a whanau may quarrel among themselves, they will unite together to work for the good of their marae in caring for their visitors.

One cannot assume that because a Maori has acquired status in the Pakeha world she or he has mana in the Maori world.

The mantle of mana embraces people and, when worn, it provides for more than just prestige and status; it is a quality that is felt rather than seen – a quality that is recognised by others rather than a status that one can work for.

An individual cannot demand that mana be bestowed upon him or her. Others recognising and wishing to acknowledge that individual's continued service to other people may in their own way show a respectful deference to him or her.

A principal of a school automatically has status in the Pakeha community. However, that same principal may not be accorded any degree of mana.

MAURI

Mauri means ethos, life force, or life principle. It applies to animate and inanimate things. For example, one may refer to "te mauri o te whare" (ethos of the house) or "te mauri o te whai korero" (life force of the speeches). Each person or object has a mauri, and the sum total of all the characteristics of a person reflects his or her personality.

The mauri of the marae is enhanced if its kawa is practised regularly and correctly. In some instances people have been known to spiritually place the mauri of their marae within an object for safekeeping. When, as has happened, the mauri is removed from the marae, either deliberately or inadvertently, the marae suffers; the tangata whenua have difficulty working together, things go wrong, and often there is a general lack of commitment and co-operation. When the mauri is replaced, the marae is again able to function to its full capacity and with the mana that it previously had. This is the main objective in ensuring that the last speaker in a whai korero situation is tangata whenua – he will retain the mauri of the marae.

For the same reason, when leaving the marae, manuhiri speak first. The tangata whenua then, again by speaking last, retain their mauri.

PAEPAE

The paepae is the area occupied by those people who are entitled to speak on behalf of the marae during a hui. The term also applies to the people themselves and to the seats they occupy. They may be those who will whai korero during a welcome or those who will act as "chairpersons" for a hui. The paepae ensures that a hui runs smoothly and that the mana of the marae is upheld.

The paepae is located in front of, or to the side of, the whare nui for a welcome on the marae-atea. Within the whare, it is the area immediately inside the doorway.

Although the occupants of the paepae may change many times during the course of a hui, the paepae itself is only vacated when people go for a meal and at night when a meeting has been concluded. It is never vacated during a tangi as long as there is a possibility that further manuhiri will arrive.

It is not for any one to automatically occupy the paepae. The mana of the marae is associated with the mana of the people of the paepae. An invitation to join them is an honour indeed.

TAHA MAORI

To speak of taha Maori is to look at things from a Maori perspective – to bring into focus attitudes that were, and in many cases still are, the bases for responses to particular circumstances. As Maori values are usually based on traditional cultural beliefs, responses often reflect a spiritual component. Attitudes are shaped by feelings and by people, rather than by individualistic and materialistic considerations.

TAPU

Tapu is often translated as "sacred" but is better explained as something that has a value that is to be respected. It places a sanction on a person, an object, or a place. Tapu is largely a matter for the individual because it requires protective and disciplinary responses. It is more than mere native superstition; it acts as a means of social control. People's possessions carry their tapu and, in the past, would therefore not be stolen – the greater the mana of the person, and the higher the value of the item, the greater the tapu.

Tapu regulates behaviour. Antisocial behaviour should not take place, because of the consequences of tapu relating to such behaviour. Some activities governed by tapu appear nothing more than common sense and the respect for people and property; others have a very deep emotional and spiritual base. Sadly, the strict controls that were previously effected by tapu have not been replaced in today's world.

Thus the prohibitions associated with the forest and the sea ensured a continuous supply of food from these sources. The rejection of such self-disciplinary prohibitions required in recent times the establishment of the New Zealand Forest Service (now the Ministry of Forestry and other agencies) and the Ministry of Agriculture and Fisheries.

TE REO MAORI

This is the Maori language.

Sometimes the majority group in a society can be hostile to any language other than their own. The marae is one place where Maori is the first language. It is not, however, the only one. In many Maori speeches the use of a few Maori words conveys a total meaning. Hence, by using the words "Papatuanuku", "nga mate" or "te ao", one conveys a spiritual significance that is understood by others who understand the language. Similarly, a phrase referring to an ancestor or a happening is understood in its entirety without the need for full explanation.

On a marae the use of Maori language by the Pakeha is appreciated and the respect that a Pakeha shows merely by learning some of the language is reciprocated by the increase in mana accorded to that person.

Maori is the cultural language of the Maori people. It is intimately intertwined with the culture that Maori people want to express. Its beauty is not only in its sound but also in its symbolism, rituals, gestures and presentation, as well as its ability within the Maori context to be expressed in song, poetry, speech-making, chants, and the haka.

"Te reo" is the essence and foundation of being Maori.

TIKANGA

Tikanga is basically the way that kawa is implemented. These procedures vary between tribal groups and even between the various marae within a tribe. Each marae evolves a system that encompasses its particular beliefs and is suitable for its people. For example, Waikato marae have their karakia in the morning and the evening as close to 7 o'clock as possible; marae that have a Ringatu affiliation have their karakia at dawn and in the evenings as close to sunrise and sunset as possible. Variations to this tikanga will be made according to what the marae people desire.

Tikanga includes all of the activities that take place on the marae or in a Maori context. For example, some allow photographs in their whare – others do not; some marae have their final hakari (feast) before the burial of the tupapaku – others return to the marae for the hakari after the burial.

TURANGAWAEWAE

This literally means a place to stand, and it indicates the rights and obligations associated with a certain place. It is a situational identity that gives a person, through genealogy or association, the right to say humbly, "I am monarch of all I survey". Turangawaewae is determined by one's iwi or hapu. It provides a home base on a marae that can give, for example, the right for a person to speak as a tangata whenua within the confines of the tuakana/teina relationship. (Normally an elder brother has precedence over a younger brother, a father over a son, and an older person over a younger person.) Turangawaewae enables a person to say with confidence, "I belong".

WAIRUA

Wairua can be thought of as spirituality. Just as there is an important relationship between life and death, so is there also a crucial relationship between people and God. The Maori acknowledges the wholeness of life in which there is an intangible presence, often referred to as God but seen also as a force over which people have no control.

The spiritual concepts of Christianity were very easy for the Maori to comprehend, because they already believed very much in both the physical and spiritual dimensions of the human being. The spiritual aspect of a person, or one's wairua, is the part that continues, even after death. It is closely related to the Christian "soul".

The acceptance of wairua provides an easy way of understanding the relationships of nature. There is a spiritual relationship between the trees and the birds. Yet the winds, the sun, and the rain affect the trees. So, then, people have a relationship with and a responsibility to the wind, the rain, the trees, the birds, the sun, each other, and a "greater force beyond".

WHAI KORERO

Whai korero means "to speak" or "to orate". A particular format will be followed by "te tohunga o te whai korero" (the expert in oratory). Although individuals will speak to their own level of ability, a few basic rules apply to the orator rather than to the oration.

At all times the kai korero will direct their remarks at the "opposition". The tangata whenua kai korero will direct their remarks at the manuhiri kai korero. If the tikanga concerning where the kai korero should sit is followed, they know automatically who these speakers will be. At all times they will keep their paepae or the whare behind them, though they may move about.

The manuhiri kai korero will speak towards the paepae or the whare, keeping their group behind them. At no time should any speaker – whether on the marae-atea or in the whare – turn his back on the opposite paepae.

When a marae-atea speech is concluded, the kai korero should be standing in such a position that those who will support him or her for the waiata do not have to walk any distance to join them.

When speaking inside the whare, stand so that there are as few people as possible behind you. In some cases it is best to move towards the centre back of the whare and face the paepae from this position; at other times you should stand on the mattress with the wall at your back.

If it is not possible to take up such a position, then apologise to those behind you for not facing them, explaining that circumstances prevent "te kanohi ki te kanohi" – an "eye to eye" situation.

People speak to people; not to others about people.

WHANAUNGATANGA

This means extended kinship ties. All those people who belong to a marae can trace their whakapapa to the marae and the ancestor it portrays. They have rights to stand and speak but they also have obligations to maintain the marae and its mana. The term may be extended also to marae visitors while they are at a hui. It is normal to address the members of a hui as a family – "Kia ora e te whanau".

The concept of whanaungatanga also has a historic dimension in that the house is normally named after an ancestor of the tribe. It is extended further by the poupou, which depict ancestors of other tribes to which visitors can relate.

WHARE MAHANA

This is literally a "warm house". Once a group goes onto a marae and occupies the whare, it is believed that the ancestral spirits return to that house and, having been appropriately acknowledged, keep the house warm. To retain this warmth, the whare should not be left empty during a hui. Often older people will remain in the whare or on the whakamahau (porch) while others are having their meals; they will eat later with the ringa wera when people begin to return to the vicinity of the whare.

Glossary

The meanings of words and phrases given here are related to the way they are used in the text. The word "te" often appears in the text, but it is not repeated in the glossary. "Te" is a definitive and generally means "the". In the text, for example, we have "te ao", which can mean "the day" or just "life".

ao	the world; day; daylight; life
aroha	love; caring for others
haere	go
haere ra	farewell
haeremai	come forward; welcome
haka	posture dance usually performed by males
hakari	a feast
hangi	food cooked in an earth oven; the actual earth oven
hapu	the extended family group with a common ancestor
harakeke	flax

hariru	to shake hands
he tipuranga	the growth of knowledge and understanding
hei whakamahana	to warm with one's presence
heke	the patterned rafters in a whare whakairo
hinengaro	the mind; a person's innermost thoughts
Hine-nui-te-po	Goddess of Death
hongi	to press noses
hui	a meeting or gathering together of people for a specific reason
hui whakamutunga	the final "session" of a hui
huihuinga ki waho	gathering together outside the marae
hunga mate	those who have died
hunga ora	those who are living
hupe	mucus
iwi	people; also refers to the wider tribal group, e.g. Te Arawa tribes, Ngapuhi tribes
kai	food; to eat; when used before a verb it means "the person who"
kai karanga	the person who is giving the karanga or call of welcome on behalf of the tangata whenua

kai korero	the speaker
kai whakautu	the person who is giving the karanga or call on behalf of the visitors
kainga tupu	the place where a person was raised
kauta	the dining room
ka pai	very good; well done
karakia	prayer
karanga	the call of welcome
karanga whakautu	the call in response
kaumatua	elders
kaupapa	topic; plan
kawa	protocol
kehua	ghosts
ki raro	to sit down
ki tona okiokinga	to his or her final resting place
ki tua o te arai	beyond the veil, when referring to death
kia tau te rangimarie	"let peace reign"
koha	gift
korero	speak; speech
kowhaiwhai	patterns on the rafters (heke) of a whare

kuia	elderly woman
kumu	backside
mahi	work; to work
maihi	the bargeboards of a whare
makutu	to lay a curse
mana	loosely translated as status or prestige
manaaki	to care for
manaakitanga	caring for others
manuhiri	visitors
Maoritanga	things that relate directly to the values and concepts of the Maori people
marae	the traditional meeting place of the Maori people
marae-atea	the area between the hosts and the guests during a welcome
marae kainga	a person's home marae
matapihi	window
mate	to die; illness
matua	parent
mauri	life force
mihi	to greet; a greeting

mokopuna	grandchild
nga taonga a nga tipuna	the knowledge that has been left to us by our ancestors
Ngati Porou	East Coast tribal group
Ngati Whatua	tribal group in the Auckland area
noa	free from tapu; common
okiokianga	resting place
ope	group
paeke	format of speeches where all the speakers of one group speak consecutively
paepae	main speakers and place where they sit
paepae tapu	the paepae is sacred because of its representation of the ancestors
Pakeha	person of fair skin
pakeke	adult
Papatuanuku	Mother Earth
paraoa	bread
paremate	those who remain with the tupapaku throughout a tangi, usually family members
pataka	traditional storehouse

patiki	the tukutuku panel design that represents the flounder, a source of food
pipi	cockle
po	darkness; night; death
poroporoaki	farewell
poupou	carved panel in a meeting house
pou tokomanawa	the central carved post in the meeting house
powhiri	to welcome; the process of welcoming
puhi	a young girl; a virgin
rakau takoto	second challenger
rakau whakaara	warning challenger
rakau whakawaha	third challenger
rangatahi	youth; young people
rangatira	leader; older adults
Rangi-e-tu-nei	the Sky Father of mythology
Ranginui	the Sky Father
reo	language; voice
rewena	bread made from potato yeast
ringa wera	"hot hands"; workers; those who care for the marae and its visitors

roimata	tears
Rongo/Rongomatane	God of Peace
rongopai	reference to the Bible; the coming of Christianity
taha Maori	Maori aspects of life
tahuhu	the ridgepole of a meeting house
taiaha	a wooden spear
take	reason; concern; topic for discussion
taki	dart or twig used for a wero
tamariki	children
Tane Mahuta	God of the Forests and Birds
Tangaroa	God of the Seas and Sea-life
tangata	man; people; male
tangata whenua	(tangata kainga, hunga kainga) people of the marae; home people
tangi	to cry; the mourning for the dead; also applies to the cry or call of a bird and the ringing of a bell
tangihanga	the ceremony of mourning the dead
taonga	those things of value to a person that have been handed down through the generations
tapu	loosely translated as "sacred"

tatau	doorway; the door
taua	warrior
tauparapara	a recitation to alert people
tautoko	to support or second
Tawhirimatea	God of Winds
Te Arawa	the tribal group in the Rotorua area
te huihuinga ki waho	the gathering together outside the marae
teina	younger relative
tekoteko	the carved figure at the top of a meeting house
te tonga o te ra	sunset
ti tree	tree used as firewood
tihei mauriora	a term used to draw attention to oneself when wishing to speak. May be variously translated as "the breath or sneeze of life", "behold, I live", "listen, I speak".
tikanga	custom; the way things are done
tikanga Maori	the Maori way of doing things
tipuna	ancestors
tipuna matua	male ancestors; grandfather
tipuna whaea	female ancestors; grandmother
Tu Matauenga	God of Fierce Man; God of War

tua o te arai	beyond the veil; those who have passed from this life
tuakana	older relative
tukua iho	let down
tukutuku	woven panels in the meeting house
tupapaku	the body of the deceased
turangawaewae	standing place from where one gains the authority to belong
tutakitanga	the act of meeting with people, usually involving physical contact
tu mai, tu atu	speeches where hosts and visitors alternate
urupa	cemetery; burial place
wahi	place
wahi tapu	a sacred place
waewae tapu	a person who is going onto a specific marae for the first time
waiata	song; to sing
waiata-a-ringa	action song
wairua	spirit; spiritual; spirituality
wero	challenge
whaea	mother or elderly female relative

whai korero	to speak; to orate; a speech
whakaeke	to go onto
whakaeke mai	come onto
whakaekenga	the act of going onto a marae
whakamahau	porch or verandah of a meeting house
whakanoa	the act of releasing from tapu
whakanui i te mana o te marae	to enhance the mana of the marae
whakapaingia nga kai	to bless the food; to say grace
whakapapa	genealogy
whakatangata whenua	the process by which visitors become tangata whenua for the duration of their stay
whanau	family
whanaungatanga	family relationship
whare	house or building
whare hui	meeting house
whare kai	dining room
whare karakia	a church
whare mahana	a warm house
whare moe	the sleeping house

whare nui	the main house or marae
whare puni	the sleeping house
whare tipuna	the ancestral house
wheke	the rafters of the house